HERSHEY'S 100th ANNIVERSARY

100 YEARS OF HERSHEY'S FAVORITES

Publications International, Ltd.

This edition published by Publications International, Ltd.,
7373 N. Cicero Ave., Lincolnwood, IL 60646.

All recipes developed and tested by the Hershey Kitchens.

Photography: Sacco Productions Limited, Chicago

Black and white photography on pages 4 and 5 courtesy of *Hershey Community Archives*.

Pictured on the front cover: *(Clockwise from top left):* Quick & Easy Fudgey Brownies *(page 96),* Fudgey German Chocolate Sandwich Cookies *(page 77),* Hershey's Lavish Chocolate Cake *(page 58),* Double-Decker Fudge *(page 21),* Chocolate Thumbprint Cookies *(page 16),* Chocolate & Vanilla Swirl Tart *(page 111).*

Pictured on the back cover: *(clockwise from top):* Hershey's White and Dark Chocolate Fudge Torte *(page 30),* Deep Dark Chocolate Cake *(page 18),* Giant Three-In-One Chocolate Chip Cookie *(page 82),* Hershey's Cocoa Cream Pie *(page 15).*

ISBN: 0-7853-0944-6

Library of Congress Catalog Card Number: 94-67969

Manufactured in U.S.A.

8 7 6 5 4 3 2 1

Nutritional Analysis: Nutritional information is given for some of the recipes in this publication. Each analysis is based on the food items in the ingredient list, except ingredients labeled as "optional." When more than one ingredient choice is listed, the first ingredient is used for analysis. If a range for the amount of an ingredient is given, nutritional analysis is based on the lowest amount. Foods offered as "serve with" suggestions are not included in the analysis unless otherwise stated.

Microwave Cooking: Microwave cooking times given in this publication are approximate. Numerous variables, such as the microwave oven's rated wattage and starting temperature, shape, amount and depth of the food, can affect cooking time. Use the cooking times as a guideline and check for doneness before adding more time. Lower-wattage ovens may consistently require longer cooking times.

 This symbol indicates that a recipe has only microwave preparation directions.

If you have questions or comments about the recipes in this publication, or about any of our fine Hershey products, please write us at the Hershey Kitchens, P.O. Box 815, Hershey, PA 17033-0815, or call us, toll-free, weekdays 9 A.M. – 4 P.M., Eastern Time, at 1-800-468-1714.

CONTENTS

THE HERSHEY STORY

Since 1894, when Milton Hershey built his chocolate factory amid the dairy farms of central Pennsylvania, the name Hershey has been synonymous with chocolate. 100 years later, Hershey Foods Corporation is committed to manufacturing food products of high quality and exceptional value. In 1994, Hershey Foods Corporation celebrates its 100th anniversary by bringing you this collection of recipes from the Hershey Kitchens. These recipes—classic favorites and newly developed recipes—all use quality Hershey®s ingredients that have been introduced to home bakers over the years.

Milton S. Hershey was raised to respect hard work and learned early to take risks. After an apprenticeship in a confectionery shop in Lancaster, Pennsylvania, he opened his own candy business in Philadelphia, which later failed. Undaunted, he began working for a Denver candy maker. There he learned a valuable lesson that would become important in his future success—fresh milk is the key to a high quality product. Mr. Hershey later returned to Pennsylvania and with borrowed money founded a successful caramel business.

In the early 1890s, Mr. Hershey became interested in the chocolate business. In 1894 he began marketing cocoa, baking chocolate, chocolate bars and novelties. Eventually he sold his caramel business, but retained the right to make chocolate. Then milk chocolate was considered a luxury item—handmade, expensive and sold only in specialty shops. Mr. Hershey, however, was confident that he could not only mass-produce milk chocolate, but make it affordable for everyone.

Remembering the lesson he learned in Denver, Mr. Hershey moved his business to the rich dairyland north of

HERSHEY'S Milk Chocolate Bar Label, 1905

Lancaster, Pennsylvania. There he could always obtain ample supplies of the fresh milk that he believed was the secret to making high quality milk chocolate.

Senior Hall of Milton Hershey School, c. 1940

With a successful business and the financial security it brought, Mr. Hershey wanted to do something for others. Therefore, in 1909 he and his wife, Catherine, created a trust fund to endow a home and school they had founded for orphan boys. Today the Milton Hershey School, on 10,000 acres in Hershey, Pennsylvania, provides housing and education for nearly 1,100 children whose family lives have been disrupted. The Milton Hershey School is a major stockholder of Hershey Foods Corporation, controls the corporation's voting shares and is a direct beneficiary of Hershey Foods' success.

In 1994, the Hershey Foods Corporation is dedicated to introducing new products that meet the needs of the ever-changing consumer while remaining committed to quality and value. As new products are introduced and people's tastes change, the Hershey Kitchens develop taste-tempting recipes for spectacular cakes, irresistible cookies and even light and low fat desserts. From the 1920s to this 100th anniversary cookbook, Hershey's recipes have

given American consumers mouthwatering ideas to make their mealtimes a little sweeter. So browse through the following pages, enjoy the enticing photography and celebrate Hershey's 100th anniversary with these luscious creations. If you have any questions or comments about these recipes or any of our fine products, please write to the Hershey Kitchens, P.O. Box 815, Hershey, PA 17033-0815 or call us, toll-free, weekdays from 9 A.M. to 4 P.M. Eastern Time at 1-800-468-1714.

HERSHEY'S KISSES Milk Chocolates, introduced 1907, HERSHEY'S KISSES WITH ALMONDS Chocolates, introduced 1990, and HERSHEY'S HUGS Chocolates and HERSHEY'S HUGS WITH ALMONDS Chocolates, introduced 1993

100 YEARS OF HERSHEY FAVORITES

Best Brownies

½ cup (1 stick) butter or
    margarine, melted
1 cup sugar
1 teaspoon vanilla extract
2 eggs
½ cup all-purpose flour

⅓ cup HERSHEY'S Cocoa
¼ teaspoon baking powder
¼ teaspoon salt
½ cup chopped nuts (optional)
    Creamy Brownie Frosting
    (recipe follows)

Heat oven to 350°F. Grease 9-inch square baking pan. In medium bowl, stir together butter, sugar and vanilla. Add eggs; with spoon, beat well. Stir together flour, cocoa, baking powder and salt. Add to egg mixture; beat until well blended. Stir in nuts, if desired. Spread batter into prepared pan. Bake 20 to 25 minutes or until brownies begin to pull away from sides of pan. Cool completely in pan on wire rack. Prepare Creamy Brownie Frosting; spread over brownies. Cut into squares.
About 16 brownies

Creamy Brownie Frosting

3 tablespoons butter or
    margarine, softened
3 tablespoons HERSHEY'S
    Cocoa
1 tablespoon light corn syrup
    or honey

½ teaspoon vanilla extract
1 cup powdered sugar
1 tablespoon milk

In small mixer bowl, beat butter, cocoa, corn syrup and vanilla until blended. Add powdered sugar and milk; beat until smooth and of spreading consistency. Add additional milk, ½ teaspoon at a time, if needed.

Top to bottom: Peanut Butter Chips and Jelly Bars (page 8), Best Brownies

Hot Fudge Pudding Cake

1¼ cups granulated sugar,
   divided
1 cup all-purpose flour
7 tablespoons HERSHEY'S
   Cocoa, divided
2 teaspoons baking powder
¼ teaspoon salt
½ cup milk

⅓ cup butter or margarine,
   melted
1½ teaspoons vanilla extract
½ cup packed light brown
   sugar
1¼ cups hot water
   Whipped topping (optional)

Heat oven to 350°F. In large bowl, stir together ¾ cup granulated sugar, flour, 3 tablespoons cocoa, baking powder and salt. Stir in milk, butter and vanilla; beat until smooth. Pour batter into 8- or 9-inch square baking pan. Stir together remaining ½ cup granulated sugar, brown sugar and remaining 4 tablespoons cocoa; sprinkle mixture evenly over batter. Pour water over top. *Do not stir.* Bake 35 to 40 minutes or until center is almost set. Cool 15 minutes; spoon into dessert dishes. Spoon sauce from bottom of pan over top of cake. Serve warm with whipped topping, if desired. Garnish as desired.   *8 servings*

Peanut Butter Chips and Jelly Bars

1½ cups all-purpose flour
½ cup sugar
¾ teaspoon baking powder
½ cup (1 stick) cold butter or
   margarine

1 egg, beaten
¾ cup grape jelly
1⅔ cups (10-ounce package)
   REESE'S Peanut Butter
   Chips, divided

Heat oven to 375°F. Grease 9-inch square baking pan. Stir together flour, sugar and baking powder; with pastry blender, cut in butter until mixture resembles coarse crumbs. Add egg; blend well. Reserve half the mixture; press remaining mixture onto bottom of prepared pan. Spread jelly over crust. Sprinkle 1 cup peanut butter chips over jelly. Stir together reserved crumb mixture with remaining ⅔ cup chips; sprinkle over top. Bake 25 to 30 minutes or until lightly browned. Cool completely in pan on wire rack. Cut into bars.   *About 16 bars*

Hot Fudge Pudding Cake

Chocolate Bavarian Pie

1 envelope unflavored gelatin
1¾ cups milk, divided
⅔ cup sugar
6 tablespoons HERSHEY'S Cocoa
1 tablespoon light corn syrup
2 tablespoons butter (do *not* use margarine)

¾ teaspoon vanilla extract
1 cup (½ pint) cold whipping cream
1 baked 9-inch pie crust *or* crumb crust

In medium saucepan, sprinkle gelatin over 1 cup milk; let stand 2 minutes to soften. Stir together sugar and cocoa. Add to mixture in saucepan. Add corn syrup. Cook, stirring constantly, until mixture comes to a boil. Remove from heat. Add butter; stir until melted. Blend in ¾ cup milk and vanilla. Pour into large mixer bowl. Cool; refrigerate until almost set. In small bowl on high speed of electric mixer, beat whipping cream until stiff. Beat chocolate mixture on medium speed of electric mixer until smooth. On low speed, add half the whipped cream to chocolate mixture, beating just until blended. Pour into prepared crust. Refrigerate 3 hours or until firm. Just before serving, garnish with remaining whipped cream. Cover; refrigerate leftover pie.   *6 to 8 servings*

Black Magic Cake

2 cups sugar
1¾ cups all-purpose flour
¾ cup HERSHEY'S Cocoa
2 teaspoons baking soda
1 teaspoon baking powder
1 teaspoon salt
2 eggs

1 cup buttermilk or sour milk*
1 cup strong black coffee *or* 2 teaspoons powdered instant coffee plus 1 cup boiling water
½ cup vegetable oil
1 teaspoon vanilla extract

To sour milk: Use 1 tablespoon white vinegar plus milk to equal 1 cup.

Heat oven to 350°F. Grease and flour two 9-inch round baking pans.** In large bowl, stir together sugar, flour, cocoa, baking soda, baking powder and salt. Add eggs, buttermilk, coffee, oil and vanilla; beat on medium speed of electric mixer 2 minutes. (Batter will be thin.) Pour batter evenly into prepared pans. Bake 30 to 35 minutes or until wooden pick inserted in center comes out clean. Cool 10 minutes; remove from pans to wire racks. Cool completely. Frost as desired.

10 to 12 servings

**One 13×9×2-inch baking pan may be substituted for 9-inch round baking pans. Prepare as directed above. Bake 35 to 40 minutes or until wooden pick inserted in center comes out clean. Cool completely in pan on wire rack. Frost as desired.

Reese's Chewy Chocolate Cookies

1¼ cups (2½ sticks) butter or
    margarine, softened
2 cups sugar
2 eggs
2 teaspoons vanilla extract
2 cups all-purpose flour

¾ cup HERSHEY'S Cocoa
1 teaspoon baking soda
½ teaspoon salt
1⅔ cups (10-ounce package)
    REESE'S Peanut Butter
    Chips

Heat oven to 350°F. In large mixer bowl, beat butter and sugar until creamy. Add eggs and vanilla; beat well. Stir together flour, cocoa, baking soda and salt; gradually add to butter mixture, beating well. Stir in peanut butter chips. Drop dough by rounded teaspoonfuls onto ungreased cookie sheet. Bake 8 to 9 minutes or until set. *Do not overbake.* (Cookies will be soft; they will puff while baking and flatten while cooling.) Cool slightly; remove from cookie sheet to wire rack. Cool completely.

About 4½ dozen cookies

Reese's Chewy Chocolate Pan Cookies: *Spread dough into greased 15½×10½×1-inch jelly-roll pan. Bake at 350°F for 20 minutes or until set. Cool completely in pan on wire rack; cut into bars. Makes about 4 dozen bars.*

Reese's Chewy Chocolate Cookie Ice Cream Sandwiches: *Prepare Reese's Chewy Chocolate Cookies as directed; cool. Place small scoop of slightly softened vanilla ice cream between flat sides of two cookies. Gently press together. Serve immediately or wrap and freeze.*

Hershey's Great American Chocolate Chip Cookies

1 cup (2 sticks) butter, softened
¾ cup granulated sugar
¾ cup packed light brown sugar
1 teaspoon vanilla extract
2 eggs

2¼ cups all-purpose flour
1 teaspoon baking soda
½ teaspoon salt
2 cups (12-ounce package) HERSHEY'S Semi-Sweet Chocolate Chips
1 cup chopped nuts (optional)

Heat oven to 375°F. In large mixer bowl, beat butter, granulated sugar, brown sugar and vanilla until creamy. Add eggs; beat well. Stir together flour, baking soda and salt; gradually add to butter mixture, beating well. Stir in chocolate chips and nuts, if desired. Drop dough by rounded teaspoonfuls onto ungreased cookie sheet. Bake 8 to 10 minutes or until lightly browned. Cool slightly; remove from cookie sheet to wire rack. Cool completely.   *About 6 dozen cookies*

Hershey's Great American Chocolate Chip Pan Cookies: *Spread dough into greased 15½×10½×1-inch jelly-roll pan. Bake at 375°F for 20 minutes or until lightly browned. Cool completely in pan on wire rack. Cut into bars. Makes about 4 dozen bars.*

Skor & Chocolate Chip Cookies: *Omit 1 cup HERSHEY'S Semi-Sweet Chocolate Chips and nuts; replace with 1 cup finely chopped SKOR bars. Drop dough onto cookie sheets and bake as directed.*

Great American Ice Cream Sandwich: *Prepare cookies as directed. Place one small scoop of slightly softened vanilla ice cream between flat sides of two cookies. Gently press together. Serve immediately or wrap and freeze.*

Top to bottom: Cocoa Kiss Cookies (page 15),
Hershey's Great American Chocolate Chip Cookies

Hershey's Cocoa Cream Pie

Hershey's Cocoa Cream Pie

½ cup HERSHEY'S Cocoa
1¼ cups sugar
⅓ cup cornstarch
¼ teaspoon salt
3 cups milk
3 tablespoons butter or
 margarine

1½ teaspoons vanilla extract
1 baked 9-inch pie crust *or*
 graham cracker crumb
 crust, cooled
Sweetened whipped cream

In medium saucepan, stir together cocoa, sugar, cornstarch and salt. Gradually add milk, stirring until smooth. Cook over medium heat, stirring constantly, until mixture comes to a boil; boil 1 minute. Remove from heat; stir in butter and vanilla. Pour into prepared crust. Press plastic wrap directly onto surface. Cool to room temperature. Refrigerate 6 to 8 hours. Serve with sweetened whipped cream. Garnish as desired. Cover; refrigerate leftover pie.   *6 to 8 servings*

Cocoa Kiss Cookies

1 cup (2 sticks) butter or
 margarine, softened
⅔ cup sugar
1 teaspoon vanilla extract
1⅔ cups all-purpose flour

¼ cup HERSHEY'S Cocoa
1 cup finely chopped pecans
1 bag (9 ounces) HERSHEY'S
 KISSES Milk Chocolates
Powdered sugar

In large bowl, beat butter, sugar and vanilla until creamy. Stir together flour and cocoa; gradually add to butter mixture, beating until blended. Add pecans; beat until well blended. Refrigerate dough about 1 hour or until firm enough to handle. Heat oven to 375°F. Remove wrappers from chocolate pieces. Mold scant tablespoon of dough around each chocolate piece, covering completely. Shape into balls. Place on ungreased cookie sheet. Bake 10 to 12 minutes or until set. Cool slightly, about 1 minute; remove from cookie sheet to wire rack. Cool completely. Roll in powdered sugar. Roll in sugar again just before serving, if desired.   *About 4½ dozen cookies*

Chocolate Thumbprint Cookies

½ cup (1 stick) butter or
   margarine, softened
⅔ cup sugar
1 egg, separated
2 tablespoons milk
1 teaspoon vanilla extract
1 cup all-purpose flour
⅓ cup HERSHEY'S Cocoa
¼ teaspoon salt

1 cup chopped nuts
Vanilla Filling (recipe
   follows)
26 HERSHEY'S KISSES Milk
   Chocolates *or* HERSHEY'S
   HUGS Chocolates *or* pecan
   halves *or* candied cherry
   halves

In small mixer bowl, beat butter, sugar, egg yolk, milk and vanilla until light and fluffy. Stir together flour, cocoa and salt; gradually add to butter mixture, beating until blended. Cover; refrigerate dough at least 1 hour or until firm enough to handle. Heat oven to 350°F. Lightly grease cookie sheet. Shape dough into 1-inch balls. With fork, beat egg white slightly. Dip each ball into egg white; roll in nuts. Place on prepared cookie sheet. Press thumb gently in center of each cookie. Bake cookies 10 to 12 minutes or until set. Meanwhile, prepare Vanilla Filling. Remove wrappers from chocolate pieces. Remove cookies from cookie sheet to wire rack; cool 5 minutes. Spoon about ¼ teaspoon prepared filling into each thumbprint. Gently press chocolate piece onto top of each cookie. Cool completely.

About 2 dozen cookies

Vanilla Filling

½ cup powdered sugar
1 tablespoon butter or
   margarine, softened

2 teaspoons milk
¼ teaspoon vanilla extract

In small bowl, combine powdered sugar, butter, milk and vanilla; beat until smooth.

Chocolate Bar Cake

1 HERSHEY'S Milk Chocolate
  Bar (7 ounces), broken
  into pieces
½ cup (1 stick) butter or
  margarine, softened
1 cup boiling water
2 cups all-purpose flour
1½ cups sugar

½ cup HERSHEY'S Cocoa
2 teaspoons baking soda
1 teaspoon salt
2 eggs
½ cup dairy sour cream
1 teaspoon vanilla extract
  Vanilla Glaze (recipe follows)

Heat oven to 350°F. Grease and flour 12-cup fluted tube pan. In small bowl, stir together chocolate, butter and water until chocolate is melted. In large mixer bowl, stir together flour, sugar, cocoa, baking soda and salt; gradually add chocolate mixture, beating on medium speed of electric mixer until well blended. Add eggs, sour cream and vanilla; blend well. Beat 1 minute. Pour batter into prepared pan. Bake 50 to 55 minutes or until wooden pick inserted in center comes out clean. Cool 10 minutes; remove from pan to wire rack. Cool completely. Prepare Vanilla Glaze; drizzle over cake.   *10 to 12 servings*

Vanilla Glaze

¼ cup (½ stick) butter or
  margarine
2 cups powdered sugar

2 tablespoons hot water
1 teaspoon vanilla extract

In medium microwave-safe bowl, place butter. Microwave at HIGH (100%) 30 seconds or until melted. Gradually stir in powdered sugar, water and vanilla; beat with whisk until smooth and slightly thickened. Add additional water, 1 teaspoon at at time, if needed.

Deep Dark Chocolate Cake

2 cups sugar
1¾ cups all-purpose flour
¾ cup HERSHEY'S Cocoa or
    HERSHEY'S European
    Style Cocoa
1½ teaspoons baking powder
1½ teaspoons baking soda
1 teaspoon salt

2 eggs
1 cup milk
½ cup vegetable oil
2 teaspoons vanilla extract
1 cup boiling water
    One-Bowl Buttercream
      Frosting (recipe follows)

Heat oven to 350°F. Grease and flour two 9-inch round baking pans.* In large mixer bowl, stir together sugar, flour, cocoa, baking powder, baking soda and salt. Add eggs, milk, oil and vanilla; beat on medium speed of electric mixer 2 minutes. Stir in water. (Batter will be thin.) Pour batter evenly into prepared pans. Bake 30 to 35 minutes or until wooden pick inserted in center comes out clean. Cool 10 minutes; remove from pans to wire racks. Cool completely. Prepare One-Bowl Buttercream Frosting; spread between layers and over top and sides of cake.

8 to 10 servings

One 13×9×2-inch baking pan may be substituted for 9-inch round baking pans. Prepare as directed above. Bake 35 to 40 minutes. Cool completely in pan on wire rack. Frost as desired.

One-Bowl Buttercream Frosting

6 tablespoons butter or
    margarine, softened
2⅔ cups powdered sugar
½ cup HERSHEY'S Cocoa or
    HERSHEY'S European
    Style Cocoa

⅓ cup milk
1 teaspoon vanilla extract

In small mixer bowl, beat butter until creamy. Add powdered sugar and cocoa alternately with milk, beating well after each addition until smooth and of spreading consistency. Blend in vanilla. Add additional milk, 1 teaspoon at a time, if needed.

Deep Dark Chocolate Cake

Top to bottom: Rich Cocoa Fudge (page 22), Double-Decker Fudge

Double-Decker Fudge

1 cup REESE'S Peanut Butter
   Chips
1 cup HERSHEY'S Semi-Sweet
   Chocolate Chips or
   HERSHEY'S MINI CHIPS
   Semi-Sweet Chocolate
2¼ cups sugar

1 jar (7 ounces) marshmallow
   creme
¾ cup evaporated milk
¼ cup (½ stick) butter or
   margarine
1 teaspoon vanilla extract

Line 8-inch square pan with foil, extending foil over edges of pan. In medium bowl, place peanut butter chips. In second medium bowl, place chocolate chips. In heavy 3-quart saucepan, combine sugar, marshmallow creme, evaporated milk and butter. Cook over medium heat, stirring constantly, until mixture comes to a boil; boil 5 minutes, stirring constantly. Remove from heat; stir in vanilla. Immediately stir half the hot mixture (1½ cups) into peanut butter chips until chips are completely melted; quickly spread into prepared pan. Stir remaining hot mixture into chocolate chips until chips are completely melted. Quickly spread over top of peanut butter layer. Cool to room temperature; refrigerate until firm. Use foil to lift fudge out of pan; peel off foil. Cut into pieces. Store in tightly covered container at room temperature.

About 5 dozen pieces or about 2 pounds fudge

Note: *For best results, do not double this recipe.*

Peanut Butter Fudge: *Omit chocolate chips; place 1⅔ cups (10-ounce package) REESE'S Peanut Butter Chips in large bowl. Cook fudge mixture as directed above. Add to chips; stir until chips are completely melted. Pour into prepared pan; cool to room temperature.*

Chocolate Fudge: *Omit peanut butter chips; place 2 cups (12-ounce package) HERSHEY'S Semi-Sweet Chocolate Chips or HERSHEY'S MINI CHIPS Semi-Sweet Chocolate in large bowl. Cook fudge mixture as directed above. Add to chips; stir until chips are completely melted. Pour into prepared pan; cool to room temperature.*

Rich Cocoa Fudge

3 cups sugar
⅔ cup HERSHEY'S Cocoa or
    HERSHEY'S European
    Style Cocoa
⅛ teaspoon salt

1½ cups milk
¼ cup (½ stick) butter or
    margarine
1 teaspoon vanilla extract

Line 8- or 9-inch square pan with foil, extending foil over edges of pan. Butter foil. In heavy 4-quart saucepan, stir together sugar, cocoa and salt; stir in milk. Cook over medium heat, stirring constantly, until mixture comes to a full rolling boil. Boil, without stirring, until mixture reaches 234°F on candy thermometer or until syrup, when dropped into very cold water, forms a soft ball that flattens when removed from water. (Bulb of thermometer should not rest on bottom of saucepan.) Remove from heat. Add butter and vanilla. *Do not stir.* Cool at room temperature to 110°F (lukewarm). Beat with wooden spoon until fudge thickens and just begins to lose some of its gloss. Quickly spread into prepared pan; cool completely. Use foil to lift fudge out of pan; peel off foil. Cut into squares. Store in tightly covered container at room temperature.

About 36 pieces or 1¾ pounds fudge

Note: *For best results, do not double this recipe.*

Nutty Rich Cocoa Fudge: *Beat cooked fudge as directed. Immediately stir in 1 cup chopped almonds, pecans or walnuts; quickly spread into prepared pan.*

Marshmallow-Nut Cocoa Fudge: *Increase cocoa to ¾ cup. Cook fudge as directed. Add 1 cup marshmallow creme with butter and vanilla. (Do not stir.) Cool to 110°F (lukewarm). Beat 10 minutes; stir in 1 cup chopped nuts. Pour into prepared pan. (Fudge will not set until poured into pan.)*

Chocolate Lover's Cheesecake

Graham Crust (recipe
follows)
2 packages (8 ounces *each*)
cream cheese, softened
¾ cup plus 2 tablespoons sugar,
divided
½ cup HERSHEY'S Cocoa

2 teaspoons vanilla extract,
divided
2 eggs
1 cup HERSHEY'S Semi-Sweet
Chocolate Chips
1 cup (8 ounces) dairy sour
cream

Prepare Graham Crust. Heat oven to 375°F. In large mixer bowl on medium speed
of electric mixer, beat cream cheese, ¾ cup sugar, cocoa and 1 teaspoon vanilla
until smooth. Add eggs; beat until blended. Stir in chocolate chips. Pour into
prepared crust. Bake 20 minutes. Remove from oven to wire rack; cool 15 minutes.
Increase oven temperature to 425°F. In small bowl, stir together sour cream,
remaining 2 tablespoons sugar and remaining 1 teaspoon vanilla; stir until
smooth. Spread over baked filling. Bake 10 minutes. Remove from oven to wire
rack. With knife, immediately loosen cake from side of pan. Cool completely;
remove side of pan. Refrigerate several hours or until cold. Cover; refrigerate
leftover cheesecake. *10 to 12 servings*

Graham Crust

1½ cups graham cracker crumbs
⅓ cup sugar

⅓ cup butter or margarine,
melted

In medium bowl, stir together crumbs, sugar and butter. Press mixture onto
bottom and halfway up side of 9-inch springform pan.

Marble Cheesecake

Marble Cheesecake

HERSHEY'S Chocolate
Crumb Crust (recipe
follows)
3 packages (8 ounces *each*)
cream cheese, softened
1 cup sugar, divided
½ cup dairy sour cream

2½ teaspoons vanilla extract,
divided
3 tablespoons all-purpose flour
3 eggs
¼ cup HERSHEY'S Cocoa
1 tablespoon vegetable oil

Prepare Hershey's Chocolate Crumb Crust. Increase oven temperature to 450°F. In large mixer bowl on medium speed of electric mixer, beat cream cheese, ¾ cup sugar, sour cream and 2 teaspoons vanilla until smooth. Gradually add flour, beating well. Add eggs, one at a time, beating well after each addition. In medium bowl, stir together cocoa and remaining ¼ cup sugar. Add oil, remaining ½ teaspoon vanilla and 1½ cups cream cheese mixture; blend well. Spoon plain and chocolate batters alternately into prepared crust, ending with spoonfuls of chocolate batter; gently swirl with knife for marbled effect. Bake 10 minutes. *Without opening door, reduce oven temperature to 250°F;* continue baking 30 minutes. Turn off oven; without opening door, leave cheesecake in oven 30 minutes. Remove from oven to wire rack. With knife, immediately loosen cheesecake from side of pan; cool completely. Refrigerate several hours or overnight; remove side of pan. Cover; refrigerate leftover cheesecake.

10 to 12 servings

Hershey's Chocolate Crumb Crust

1¼ cups vanilla wafer crumbs
(about 40 wafers)
⅓ cup powdered sugar

⅓ cup HERSHEY'S Cocoa
¼ cup (½ stick) butter or
margarine, melted

Heat oven to 350°F. In medium bowl, stir together crumbs, powdered sugar and cocoa; blend in butter. Press mixture onto bottom and ½ inch up side of 9-inch springform pan. Bake 8 minutes; cool completely.

Hot Cocoa

½ cup sugar
¼ cup HERSHEY'S Cocoa
   Dash salt
⅓ cup hot water
4 cups (1 quart) milk

¾ teaspoon vanilla extract
   Miniature marshmallows *or*
   sweetened whipped cream
   (optional)

In medium saucepan, stir together sugar, cocoa and salt; stir in water. Cook over medium heat, stirring constantly, until mixture comes to a boil. Boil 2 minutes, stirring constantly. Add milk; heat to serving temperature, stirring constantly. *Do not boil.* Remove from heat; add vanilla. Beat with rotary beater or whisk until foamy. Serve topped with marshmallows or sweetened whipped cream, if desired.

5 (8-ounce) servings

Spiced Cocoa: *Add ⅛ teaspoon ground cinnamon and ⅛ teaspoon ground nutmeg with vanilla. Serve with cinnamon stick, if desired.*

Mint Cocoa: *Add ½ teaspoon mint extract or 3 tablespoons crushed hard peppermint candy or 2 to 3 tablespoons white creme de menthe with vanilla. Serve with peppermint candy stick, if desired.*

Citrus Cocoa: *Add ½ teaspoon orange extract or 2 to 3 tablespoons orange liqueur with vanilla.*

Swiss Mocha: *Add 2 to 2½ teaspoons powdered instant coffee with vanilla.*

Canadian Cocoa: *Add ½ teaspoon maple extract with vanilla.*

Cocoa Au Lait: *Omit marshmallows or sweetened whipped cream. Spoon 2 tablespoons softened vanilla ice cream on top of each cup of cocoa at serving time.*

Slim-Trim Cocoa: *Omit sugar. Substitute skim milk for milk. Proceed as above. Stir in sugar substitute with sweetening equivalence of ½ cup sugar with vanilla.*

Quick Microwave Cocoa: *To make one serving, in microwave-safe cup or mug, combine 1 heaping teaspoon HERSHEY'S Cocoa, 2 heaping teaspoons sugar and dash of salt. Add 2 teaspoons cold milk; stir until smooth. Fill cup with milk. Microwave at HIGH (100%) 1 to 1½ minutes or until hot. Stir to blend.*

Top to bottom: Hot Cocoa, Brownie Pie à la Mode (page 28)

Brownie Pie à la Mode

½ cup sugar
2 tablespoons butter or
    margarine
2 tablespoons water
1⅓ cups HERSHEY'S Semi-
    Sweet Chocolate Chips
2 eggs
⅔ cup all-purpose flour

¼ teaspoon baking soda
¼ teaspoon salt
1 teaspoon vanilla extract
¾ cup chopped nuts (optional)
    Fudge Sauce (recipe follows,
    optional)
    Ice cream, any flavor

Heat oven to 350°F. Grease 9-inch pie plate. In medium saucepan, combine sugar, butter and water. Cook over medium heat, stirring occasionally, just until mixture comes to a boil. Remove from heat. Immediately add chocolate chips; stir until melted. Add eggs; beat with spoon until well blended. Stir together flour, baking soda and salt. Add to chocolate mixture; stir until well blended. Stir in vanilla and nuts, if desired; pour into prepared pie plate. Bake 25 to 30 minutes or until almost set. (Pie will not test done in center.) Cool. Prepare Fudge Sauce, if desired. Top warm pie with scoops of ice cream and prepared sauce.   *8 to 10 servings*

Fudge Sauce

1 cup HERSHEY'S Semi-Sweet
    Chocolate Chips
½ cup evaporated milk

¼ cup sugar
1 tablespoon butter or
    margarine

In medium microwave-safe bowl, combine all ingredients. Microwave at HIGH (100%) 1 minute; stir. If necessary, microwave at HIGH an additional 15 seconds at a time, stirring after each heating, just until chips are melted and mixture is smooth.

Chocolatetown Special Cake

½ cup HERSHEY'S Cocoa or
    HERSHEY'S European
    Style Cocoa
½ cup boiling water
⅔ cup shortening
1¾ cups sugar
1 teaspoon vanilla extract
2 eggs

2¼ cups all-purpose flour
1½ teaspoons baking soda
½ teaspoon salt
1⅓ cups buttermilk or sour
    milk*
One-Bowl Buttercream
    Frosting (page 18)

*To sour milk: Use 4 teaspoons white vinegar plus milk to equal 1⅓ cups.

Heat oven to 350°F. Grease and flour two 9-inch round baking pans. In small bowl, stir together cocoa and water until smooth. In large mixer bowl, beat shortening, sugar and vanilla until creamy. Add eggs; beat well. Stir together flour, baking soda and salt; add to shortening mixture alternately with buttermilk, beating well after each addition. Add cocoa mixture; beat well. Pour batter evenly into prepared pans. Bake 35 to 40 minutes or until wooden pick inserted in center comes out clean. Cool 10 minutes; remove from pans to wire racks. Cool completely. Prepare One-Bowl Buttercream Frosting; spread between layers and over top and sides of cake. *8 to 10 servings*

Foolproof Dark Chocolate Fudge

3 cups (1½ packages,
    12 ounces each)
    HERSHEY'S Semi-Sweet
    Chocolate Chips

1 can (14 ounces) sweetened
    condensed milk (*not*
    evaporated milk)
Dash salt
1 cup chopped walnuts
1½ teaspoons vanilla extract

Line 8- or 9-inch square pan with foil, extending foil over edges of pan. In medium, heavy saucepan over low heat, melt chocolate chips with sweetened condensed milk and salt. Remove from heat; stir in walnuts and vanilla. Spread into prepared pan. Refrigerate 2 hours or until firm. Use foil to lift fudge from pan; peel off foil. Cut into squares. Store loosely covered at room temperature. *About 5 dozen pieces or 2 pounds fudge*

Hershey's White and Dark Chocolate Fudge Torte

1 cup (2 sticks) butter or
   margarine, melted
1½ cups sugar
1 teaspoon vanilla extract
3 eggs, separated
⅔ cup HERSHEY'S Cocoa
½ cup all-purpose flour
3 tablespoons water

1⅔ cups (10-ounce package)
   HERSHEY'S Vanilla Milk
   Chips, divided
⅛ teaspoon cream of tartar
Satiny Glaze (page 32)
White Decorator Drizzle
   (page 32)

Heat oven to 350°F. Line bottom of 9-inch springform pan with foil; grease foil and side of pan. In large mixer bowl, combine butter, sugar and vanilla; beat well. Add egg yolks, one at a time, beating well after each addition. Blend in cocoa, flour and water. Stir in 1⅓ cups vanilla milk chips. Reserve remaining chips for drizzle. In small mixer bowl, beat egg whites with cream of tartar until stiff peaks form; fold into chocolate mixture. Pour batter into prepared pan. Bake 45 minutes or until top begins to crack slightly. (Cake will not test done in center.) Cool 1 hour. Cover; refrigerate until firm. Remove side of pan. Prepare Satiny Glaze and White Decorator Drizzle. Pour prepared glaze over torte; spread evenly over top and side. Decorate top of torte with prepared drizzle.* Cover; refrigerate until serving time. Refrigerate leftover torte. *10 to 12 servings*

*To decorate, drizzle with spoon or place in pastry bag with writing tip.

continued on page 32

Hershey's White and Dark Chocolate Fudge Torte

Hershey's White and Dark Chocolate Fudge Torte (continued)

Satiny Glaze

1 cup HERSHEY'S Semi-Sweet   ¼ cup whipping cream
   Chocolate Chips

In small microwave-safe bowl, place chocolate chips and whipping cream. Microwave at HIGH (100%) 1 minute; stir. If necessary, microwave at HIGH an additional 15 seconds at a time, stirring after each heating, just until chips are melted when stirred. Cool until lukewarm and slightly thickened.

White Decorator Drizzle

⅓ cup HERSHEY'S Vanilla   2 teaspoons shortening (do
   Milk Chips (reserved from   *not* use butter, margarine
   torte)   or oil)

In small microwave-safe bowl, place vanilla milk chips and shortening. Microwave at HIGH (100%) 20 to 30 seconds; stir. If necessary, microwave at HIGH an additional 15 seconds at a time, stirring after each heating, just until chips are melted when stirred.

Butterscotch Cheesecake with Chocolate Drizzle

Graham Cracker Crust   2 tablespoons milk
   (recipe follows)   4 eggs
3 packages (8 ounces *each*)   Chocolate Drizzle (recipe
   cream cheese, softened   follows)
½ cup sugar
2 tablespoons all-purpose flour
1⅔ cups (10-ounce package)
   HERSHEY'S Butterscotch
   Chips

Prepare Graham Cracker Crust. *Increase oven temperature to 350°F.* In large mixer bowl on medium speed of electric mixer, beat cream cheese, sugar and flour until smooth. In small microwave-safe bowl, place butterscotch chips and milk. Microwave at HIGH (100%) 1 minute; stir. If necessary, microwave at HIGH an additional 15 seconds at a time, stirring after each heating, just until chips are melted when stirred. Blend butterscotch mixture into cream cheese mixture. Add eggs, one at a time, blending well after each addition. Pour mixture over prepared crust. Bake 40 to 45 minutes or until almost set in center. Remove from oven to wire rack. With knife, immediately loosen cake from side of pan. Cool completely; remove side of pan. Prepare Chocolate Drizzle; drizzle over cheesecake. Refrigerate leftover cheesecake.   *12 servings*

Graham Cracker Crust

1 cup graham cracker crumbs	3 tablespoons butter or
3 tablespoons sugar	margarine, melted

Heat oven to 325°F. In small bowl, stir together crumbs, sugar and butter. Press mixture onto bottom of 9-inch springform pan. Bake 10 minutes. Cool completely.

Chocolate Drizzle

½ cup HERSHEY'S Semi-Sweet Chocolate Chips	1 tablespoon shortening (do *not* use butter, margarine or oil)

In small microwave-safe bowl, place chocolate chips and shortening. Microwave at HIGH (100%) 30 seconds; stir. If necessary, microwave at HIGH an additional 15 seconds at a time, stirring after each heating, just until chips are melted when stirred.

Top to bottom: Peanut Butter Chip Pound Cake with Streusel Swirl (page 36), Chocolate Glazed Citrus Poppy Seed Cake (page 37), Mini Chip Harvest Ring

Mini Chip Harvest Ring

¾ cup whole-wheat flour*
¾ cup all-purpose flour
¾ cup granulated sugar
½ cup packed light brown
    sugar
2 teaspoons ground cinnamon
1¼ teaspoons baking soda
½ teaspoon salt
3 eggs
¾ cup vegetable oil

1½ teaspoons vanilla extract
2 cups grated carrots, apples
    or zucchini, drained
¾ cup HERSHEY'S MINI
    CHIPS Semi-Sweet
    Chocolate
½ cup chopped walnuts
    Cream Cheese Glaze (recipe
    follows)

All-purpose flour may be substituted for whole-wheat flour.

Heat oven to 350°F. Grease and flour 6- or 8-cup fluted tube pan. In large bowl, stir together whole-wheat flour, all-purpose flour, granulated sugar, brown sugar, cinnamon, baking soda and salt. In small bowl, beat eggs, oil and vanilla. Add to dry ingredients; blend well. Stir in carrots, small chocolate chips and walnuts. Pour batter into prepared pan. Bake 45 to 50 minutes or until wooden pick inserted in center comes out clean. Cool 30 minutes; remove from pan to wire rack. Prepare Cream Cheese Glaze; spread over top of cake, allowing glaze to run down sides. Garnish as desired.   *8 to 10 servings*

Cream Cheese Glaze

1½ ounces (½ of 3-ounce
    package) cream cheese,
    softened

¾ cup powdered sugar
2 teaspoons milk
½ teaspoon vanilla extract

In small bowl, beat cream cheese, powdered sugar, milk and vanilla until smooth and of desired consistency. Add additional milk, ½ teaspoon at a time, if needed.

Peanut Butter Chip Pound Cake with Streusel Swirl

Streusel Swirl (recipe follows)
¾ cup (1½ sticks) butter or margarine, softened
1½ cups sugar
3 eggs
1 teaspoon vanilla extract
3 cups all-purpose flour
1½ teaspoons baking powder
1½ teaspoons baking soda
¼ teaspoon salt
1½ cups (12 ounces) dairy sour cream
1⅔ cups (10-ounce package) REESE'S Peanut Butter Chips
Peanut Butter Creme Glaze (recipe follows)

Prepare Streusel Swirl. Heat oven to 350°F. Grease 12-cup fluted tube pan. In large mixer bowl, beat butter, sugar, eggs and vanilla until light and fluffy. Stir together flour, baking powder, baking soda and salt; add alternately with sour cream to butter mixture, beating well after each addition. Stir in peanut butter chips. Spread half the batter into prepared pan. Sprinkle Streusel Swirl over batter. Carefully spread remaining batter over top. Bake 1 hour 5 minutes to 1 hour 10 minutes or until top is golden brown and wooden pick inserted in center comes out clean. Cool 15 minutes; remove from pan to wire rack. Cool completely. Prepare Peanut Butter Creme Glaze; drizzle over cake. Garnish as desired.

10 to 12 servings

Streusel Swirl

¼ cup packed brown sugar
¼ cup chopped nuts
½ teaspoon ground cinnamon

In small bowl, stir together brown sugar, nuts and cinnamon.

Peanut Butter Creme Glaze

⅓ cup sugar
¼ cup water
1 cup REESE'S Peanut Butter Chips
2 tablespoons marshmallow creme

In small saucepan, heat sugar and water until mixture comes to a boil. Remove from heat. Immediately add peanut butter chips; stir until melted. Add marshmallow creme; beat until smooth and of desired consistency. Add additional hot water, 1 teaspoon at a time, if needed.

Chocolate Glazed Citrus Poppy Seed Cake

1 package (about 18 ounces) lemon cake mix
⅓ cup poppy seed
⅓ cup milk
3 eggs
1 container (8 ounces) plain lowfat yogurt

1 teaspoon freshly grated lemon peel
Chocolate Citrus Glaze (recipe follows)

Heat oven to 350°F. Grease and flour 12-cup fluted tube pan or 10-inch tube pan. In large mixer bowl, combine cake mix, poppy seed, milk, eggs, yogurt and lemon peel; beat until well blended. Pour batter into prepared pan. Bake 40 to 45 minutes or until wooden pick inserted in center comes out clean. Cool 20 minutes; remove from pan to wire rack. Cool completely. Prepare Chocolate Citrus Glaze; spoon over cake, allowing glaze to run down sides. *10 to 12 servings*

Chocolate Citrus Glaze

2 tablespoons butter or margarine
2 tablespoons HERSHEY'S Cocoa or HERSHEY'S European Style Cocoa

2 tablespoons water
1 tablespoon orange-flavored liqueur (optional)
½ teaspoon orange extract
1¼ to 1½ cups powdered sugar

In small saucepan over medium heat, melt butter. With whisk, stir in cocoa and water until mixture thickens slightly. Remove from heat; stir in liqueur, if desired, orange extract and 1¼ cups powdered sugar. Whisk until smooth. If glaze is too thin, whisk in remaining ¼ cup powdered sugar. Use immediately.

German Chocolate Cheesecake

Coconut-Pecan Graham
    Crust (recipe follows)
4 bars (1 ounce *each*)
    HERSHEY'S Semi-Sweet
    Baking Chocolate, broken
    into pieces
3 packages (8 ounces *each*)
    cream cheese, softened

¾ cup sugar
½ cup dairy sour cream
2 teaspoons vanilla extract
2 tablespoons all-purpose flour
3 eggs
    Coconut-Pecan Topping
    (page 40)

Prepare Coconut-Pecan Graham Crust. *Increase oven temperature to 450°F.* In small microwave-safe bowl, place chocolate. Microwave at HIGH (100%) 1 to 1½ minutes or until chocolate is melted and smooth when stirred. In large mixer bowl on medium speed of electric mixer, beat cream cheese, sugar, sour cream and vanilla until smooth. Add flour; blend well. Add eggs and melted chocolate; beat until blended. Pour into prepared crust. Bake 10 minutes. *Without opening oven door, reduce oven temperature to 250°F.* Continue baking 35 minutes. Remove from oven to wire rack. With knife, immediately loosen cake from side of pan. Cool completely; remove side of pan. Prepare Coconut-Pecan Topping; spread over cheesecake. Refrigerate several hours. Garnish as desired. Cover; refrigerate leftover cheesecake.
10 to 12 servings

Coconut-Pecan Graham Crust

1 cup graham cracker crumbs
2 tablespoons sugar
⅓ cup butter or margarine,
    melted

¼ cup MOUNDS Sweetened
    Coconut Flakes
¼ cup chopped pecans

Heat oven to 350°F. In small bowl, combine graham cracker crumbs and sugar. Stir in butter, coconut and pecans. Press mixture onto bottom and ½ inch up side of 9-inch springform pan. Bake 8 to 10 minutes or until lightly browned. Cool completely.

continued on page 40

Top to bottom: German Chocolate Cheesecake, Sour Cherry Cheesecake with Macadamia Nut Crust (page 40)

German Chocolate Cheesecake (continued)

Coconut-Pecan Topping

½ cup (1 stick) butter or margarine
¼ cup packed light brown sugar
2 tablespoons light cream

2 tablespoons light corn syrup
1 cup MOUNDS Sweetened Coconut Flakes
½ cup chopped pecans
1 teaspoon vanilla extract

In small saucepan, melt butter; add brown sugar, light cream and corn syrup. Cook over medium heat, stirring constantly, until smooth and bubbly. Remove from heat. Stir in coconut, pecans and vanilla. Cool slightly.

Sour Cherry Cheesecake with Macadamia Nut Crust

Macadamia Nut Crust (recipe follows)
1 can (16 ounces) tart red pitted cherries
3 packages (8 ounces *each*) cream cheese, softened
1 cup sugar
3 eggs

1 teaspoon vanilla extract
1⅔ cups (10-ounce package) HERSHEY'S Vanilla Milk Chips
Sour Cherry Sauce (recipe follows)
Chopped macadamia nuts (optional)

Heat oven to 350°F. Prepare Macadamia Nut Crust. Thoroughly drain cherries, reserving liquid for sauce. Chop cherries; drain again. In large mixer bowl on medium speed of electric mixer, beat cream cheese until smooth. Add sugar, eggs and vanilla; beat until blended. In medium microwave-safe bowl, place vanilla milk chips. Microwave at HIGH (100%) 1 minute; stir. If necessary, microwave at HIGH an additional 15 seconds at a time, stirring after each heating, just until chips are melted when stirred. Blend into cream cheese mixture. Stir in chopped cherries. Pour mixture over prepared crust. Bake 50 to 55 minutes or until almost set in center. Remove from oven to wire rack. With knife, immediately loosen cake from side of pan. Cool completely; remove side of pan. Refrigerate about 3 hours. Meanwhile, prepare Sour Cherry Sauce; spoon over cheesecake. Garnish with chopped macadamia nuts, if desired. Cover; refrigerate leftover cheesecake.

10 to 12 servings

Macadamia Nut Crust

1 jar (3½ ounces) macadamia
    nuts, very finely chopped
¾ cup graham cracker crumbs

2 tablespoons sugar
¼ cup (½ stick) butter or
    margarine, melted

In medium bowl, combine macadamia nuts, crumbs, sugar and butter. Press mixture firmly onto bottom of 9-inch springform pan. Bake at 350°F for 8 minutes. Cool completely.

Sour Cherry Sauce

1 tablespoon cornstarch
    Reserved cherry juice (from
    cheesecake)

2 tablespoons cherry brandy
    or ½ teaspoon almond
    extract (optional)

In medium saucepan, combine cornstarch and cherry juice. Cook over medium heat, stirring constantly, until mixture comes to a boil and thickens. Remove from heat; stir in brandy, if desired. Cool.

Chocolate Strawberry Whipped Cream Cake

3 eggs
1 cup granulated sugar
⅓ cup water
1 teaspoon vanilla extract
¾ cup all-purpose flour
¼ cup HERSHEY'S Cocoa or
    HERSHEY'S European
    Style Cocoa

1 teaspoon baking powder
½ teaspoon salt
Powdered sugar
Strawberry Whipped Cream
    Filling (recipe follows)
Royal Glaze (page 44)

Heat oven to 375°F. Grease 15½×10½×1-inch jelly-roll pan. Line with wax paper; grease paper. In large mixer bowl on high speed of electric mixer, beat eggs until very thick and cream colored, about 5 minutes; gradually beat in granulated sugar. With mixer on low speed, beat in water and vanilla. Stir together flour, cocoa, baking powder and salt; gradually add to egg mixture, beating just until blended. Pour into prepared pan. Bake 10 to 13 minutes or until wooden pick inserted in center comes out clean. Immediately invert pan onto towel sprinkled with powdered sugar; carefully peel off wax paper. Invert cake onto wire rack covered with wax paper. Cool completely. Prepare Strawberry Whipped Cream Filling. Cut cake crosswise into four equal pieces, each about 10×3½ inches. Divide filling into thirds; spread evenly on three rectangles, leaving one plain rectangle for top. Cover and refrigerate until firm. To assemble, stack layers on top of each other with plain cake layer on top. Prepare Royal Glaze; spread over top. Refrigerate until serving. Cut into slices; refrigerate leftover cake.

8 to 10 servings

Strawberry Whipped Cream Filling

1 cup rinsed, hulled and sliced
    fresh strawberries
¼ cup HERSHEY'S Strawberry
    Flavored Syrup

1 envelope unflavored gelatin
1 cup (½ pint) cold whipping
    cream

continued on page 44

Chocolate Strawberry Whipped Cream Cake

Chocolate Strawberry Whipped Cream Cake (continued)

In food processor or blender, purée strawberries with syrup; sprinkle gelatin over mixture. Let stand until gelatin is softened, about 2 minutes; purée again for several seconds. Pour into medium microwave-safe bowl; microwave at HIGH (100%) 30 seconds to 1 minute, until mixture is hot, not boiling, and gelatin is dissolved. Cool to room temperature. In small mixer bowl on high speed of electric mixer, beat whipping cream until stiff; fold in strawberry mixture.

Royal Glaze

⅔ cup HERSHEY'S Semi-Sweet Chocolate Chips

¼ cup whipping cream

In small microwave-safe bowl, place chocolate chips and whipping cream. Microwave at HIGH (100%) 30 seconds; stir. If necessary, microwave at HIGH an additional 15 seconds at a time, stirring after each heating, just until chips are melted when stirred. Cool slightly until thickened, 5 to 10 minutes.

Frosted Peanut Butter Cake Squares

About 30 REESE'S Peanut Butter Cup Miniatures
⅓ cup butter or margarine, softened
½ cup REESE'S Creamy or Crunchy Peanut Butter
⅓ cup granulated sugar
⅓ cup packed light brown sugar

½ cup milk
2 eggs
1 teaspoon vanilla extract
1 cup all-purpose flour
1 teaspoon baking soda
¼ teaspoon salt
Chocolate Peanut Butter Topping (recipe follows)

Heat oven to 350°F. Remove wrappers from candies. Chop candies into pieces. Grease 13×9×2-inch baking pan. In small mixer bowl, beat butter, peanut butter, granulated sugar and brown sugar until well blended. Gradually add milk, eggs and vanilla, beating until smooth and well blended. Stir together flour, baking soda and salt. Add to butter mixture; beat until well blended. Spread batter into prepared pan. Bake 18 to 20 minutes or until wooden pick inserted in center comes out clean. Cool completely in pan on wire rack. Prepare Chocolate Peanut Butter Topping; spread over cake. Sprinkle candy pieces over top. Cut into squares.

12 to 14 squares

Chocolate Peanut Butter Topping

½ cup HERSHEY'S Semi-Sweet Chocolate Chips

⅓ cup REESE'S Creamy Peanut Butter

2 tablespoons butter or margarine

¼ cup powdered sugar

In medium microwave-safe bowl, place chocolate chips, peanut butter and butter. Microwave at HIGH (100%) 1 minute; stir. If necessary, microwave at HIGH an additional 15 seconds at a time, stirring after each addition, just until chips are melted when stirred. Add powdered sugar; whisk until smooth and of spreading consistency.

Cocoa Sour Cream Bundt Cake

¾ cup (1½ sticks) butter or margarine, softened

1⅔ cups sugar

2 eggs

1 teaspoon vanilla extract

¾ cup dairy sour cream

2 cups all-purpose flour

⅔ cup HERSHEY'S Cocoa

½ teaspoon salt

2 teaspoons baking soda

1 cup buttermilk or sour milk*

To sour milk: Use 1 tablespoon white vinegar plus milk to equal 1 cup.

Heat oven to 350°F. Grease and flour 9- or 12-cup fluted tube pan. In large mixer bowl on medium speed of electric mixer, beat butter, sugar, eggs and vanilla until light and fluffy; blend in sour cream. Stir together flour, cocoa and salt. Stir baking soda into buttermilk; add alternately with dry ingredients to butter mixture, beating well after each addition. Beat an additional 2 minutes. Pour into prepared pan. Bake 45 to 50 minutes or until wooden pick inserted in cake comes out clean. Cool 10 minutes; remove from pan to wire rack. Cool completely. Glaze as desired.

10 to 12 servings

Clockwise from top left: Double Chocolate Cocoa Cupcakes, Chocolate Mint Pound Cake (page 48), Cocoa Marble Gingerbread

Double Chocolate Cocoa Cupcakes

¾ cup shortening
1¼ cups granulated sugar
2 eggs
1 teaspoon vanilla extract
1¾ cups all-purpose flour
½ cup HERSHEY'S Cocoa
1 teaspoon baking soda

½ teaspoon salt
1 cup milk
1 cup HERSHEY'S MINI
    CHIPS Semi-Sweet
    Chocolate
Powdered sugar

Heat oven to 375°F. Line muffin cups (2½ inches in diameter) with paper bake cups. In large mixer bowl, beat shortening and granulated sugar until light and fluffy. Add eggs and vanilla; beat well. Stir together flour, cocoa, baking soda and salt; add alternately with milk to shortening mixture, beating well after each addition. Stir in small chocolate chips. Fill prepared muffin cups about ¾ full with batter. Bake 20 to 25 minutes or until cupcake springs back when touched lightly in center. Remove from pans to wire racks. Cool completely. Sift powdered sugar over tops of cupcakes. *About 2 dozen cupcakes*

Cocoa Marble Gingerbread

½ cup shortening
1 cup sugar
1 cup light molasses
2 eggs
1 teaspoon baking soda
1 cup boiling water
2 cups all-purpose flour
1 teaspoon salt

¼ cup HERSHEY'S Cocoa
½ teaspoon ground cinnamon
½ teaspoon ground ginger
¼ teaspoon ground cloves
¼ teaspoon ground nutmeg
    Sweetened whipped cream
    (optional)

Heat oven to 350°F. Grease and flour 13×9×2-inch baking pan. In large mixer bowl, beat shortening, sugar and molasses until blended. Add eggs; beat well. Stir baking soda into water to dissolve; add to shortening mixture alternately with combined flour and salt, beating well after each addition. Remove 2 cups

continued on page 48

Cocoa Marble Gingerbread (continued)

batter to medium bowl. Add cocoa; blend well. Add spices to remaining batter in large mixer bowl. Alternately spoon batters into prepared pan; gently swirl with knife for marbled effect. Bake 40 to 45 minutes or until wooden pick inserted in center comes out clean. Serve warm or at room temperature with sweetened whipped cream, if desired. *10 to 12 servings*

Chocolate Mint Pound Cake

½ cup (1 stick) butter or
    margarine, softened
4 ounces (½ of 8-ounce
    package) cream cheese,
    softened
¾ cup sugar
2 eggs
1 teaspoon vanilla extract

1 cup all-purpose flour
1 teaspoon baking powder
1 cup HERSHEY'S Mint
    Chocolate Chips
3 to 4 drops green food color
    (optional)
Mint Chocolate Chip Glaze
    (recipe follows, optional)

Heat oven to 325°F. Grease and flour 9×5×2¾-inch loaf pan. In small mixer bowl, beat butter, cream cheese and sugar until light and fluffy. Add eggs and vanilla; beat well. Blend in combined flour and baking powder; stir in mint chocolate chips and green food color, if desired. Pour batter into prepared pan. Bake 45 to 50 minutes or until cake pulls away from sides of pan. Cool 10 minutes; remove from pan to wire rack. Cool completely. Prepare Mint Chocolate Chip Glaze, if desired; spread over top of cake, allowing glaze to run down sides. Cool completely.

8 to 10 servings

Mint Chocolate Chip Glaze

⅔ cup HERSHEY'S Mint
    Chocolate Chips

2 tablespoons shortening (do
    not use butter, margarine
    or oil)

In small microwave-safe bowl, place mint chocolate chips and shortening. Microwave at HIGH (100%) 30 seconds; stir. If necessary, microwave at HIGH an additional 15 seconds at a time, stirring after each heating, just until chips are melted when stirred.

Chocolate Mousse Torte

⅔ cup butter or margarine,
    softened
1 cup sugar
3 eggs
1½ teaspoons vanilla extract
2 cups all-purpose flour
⅔ cup HERSHEY'S Cocoa or
    HERSHEY'S European
    Style Cocoa

1½ teaspoons baking powder
½ teaspoon baking soda
1⅓ cups milk
    Chocolate Mousse Filling
    (recipe follows)

Heat oven to 350°F. Line 15½×10½×1-inch jelly-roll pan with foil; grease and flour foil. In large bowl, beat butter and sugar until creamy. Add eggs and vanilla; beat well. Stir together flour, cocoa, baking powder and baking soda; add to butter mixture alternately with milk, beating well after each addition. Spread batter into prepared pan. Bake 15 to 20 minutes or until wooden pick inserted in center comes out clean. Cool cake in pan 10 minutes. Invert onto wire rack; carefully peel off foil. Cool completely. Prepare Chocolate Mousse Filling. Trim cake edges; cut cake crosswise into four equal pieces, each about 10×3½ inches. Place one layer on serving plate; spread with about ½ cup filling. Repeat with two more layers and filling; pipe or spread remaining filling on fourth layer. Refrigerate until ready to serve. Cover; refrigerate leftover cake.

10 to 12 servings

Chocolate Mousse Filling

1 teaspoon unflavored gelatin
1 tablespoon cold water
2 tablespoons boiling water
1 cup (½ pint) cold whipping
    cream

⅓ cup powdered sugar
3 tablespoons HERSHEY'S
    Cocoa or HERSHEY'S
    European Style Cocoa
1 teaspoon vanilla extract

In small cup, sprinkle gelatin over cold water; let stand 2 minutes to soften. Add boiling water; stir until gelatin is completely dissolved and mixture is clear. Cool 5 minutes. In large mixer bowl on high speed of electric mixer, beat whipping cream, powdered sugar, cocoa and vanilla until thickened. Add gelatin mixture; beat until stiff. Use immediately.

Triple Layer Cheesecake

LUSCIOUS COLLECTIBLE CAKES

Triple Layer Cheesecake

Chocolate Crumb Crust
(recipe follows)
3 packages (8 ounces *each*)
cream cheese, softened
¾ cup sugar
3 eggs
⅓ cup dairy sour cream
3 tablespoons all-purpose flour
1 teaspoon vanilla extract
¼ teaspoon salt

1 cup HERSHEY'S
Butterscotch Chips,
melted*
1 cup HERSHEY'S Semi-Sweet
Chocolate Chips, melted*
1 cup HERSHEY'S Vanilla
Milk Chips, melted*
Triple Drizzle (page 52,
optional)

To melt chips: Place chips in separate medium microwave-safe bowls. Microwave at HIGH (100%) 1 minute; stir. If necessary, microwave at HIGH an additional 15 seconds at a time, stirring after each heating, just until chips are melted when stirred.

Heat oven to 350°F. Prepare Chocolate Crumb Crust. In large mixer bowl on medium speed of electric mixer, beat cream cheese and sugar until smooth. Add eggs, sour cream, flour, vanilla and salt; beat until blended. Stir 1⅓ cups batter into melted butterscotch chips until smooth; pour into prepared crust. Stir 1⅓ cups batter into melted chocolate chips until smooth; pour over butterscotch layer. Stir remaining batter into melted vanilla milk chips until smooth; pour over chocolate layer. Bake 55 to 60 minutes or until almost set in center. Remove from oven to wire rack. With knife, immediately loosen cake from side of pan. Cool completely; remove side of pan. Prepare Triple Drizzle, if desired; drizzle, one flavor at a time, over top of cheesecake. Refrigerate about 3 hours. Cover; refrigerate leftover cheesecake.   *12 to 14 servings*

Chocolate Crumb Crust

1½ cups vanilla wafer crumbs
(about 45 wafers)
½ cup powdered sugar

¼ cup HERSHEY'S Cocoa
⅓ cup butter or margarine,
melted

continued on page 52

Triple Layer Cheesecake (continued)

In medium bowl, stir together crumbs, powdered sugar and cocoa; stir in butter. Press mixture onto bottom and 1½ inches up side of 9-inch springform pan. Bake at 350°F for 8 minutes. Cool completely.

Triple Drizzle

1 tablespoon *each* HERSHEY'S Butterscotch Chips, HERSHEY'S Semi-Sweet Chocolate Chips *and* HERSHEY'S Vanilla Milk Chips	1½ teaspoons shortening (do *not* use butter, margarine or oil), divided

In small microwave-safe bowl, place butterscotch chips and ½ teaspoon shortening. Microwave at HIGH (100%) 30 seconds; stir. If necessary, microwave on HIGH an additional 15 seconds at a time, stirring after each heating, just until chips are melted when stirred. Repeat procedure with chocolate chips and vanilla milk chips using ½ teaspoon shortening for each.

Quick Chocolate Cupcakes

1½ cups all-purpose flour	1 cup water
¾ cup sugar	¼ cup vegetable oil
¼ cup HERSHEY'S Cocoa	1 tablespoon white vinegar
1 teaspoon baking soda	1 teaspoon vanilla extract
½ teaspoon salt	

Heat oven to 375°F. Line muffin cups (2½ inches in diameter) with paper bake cups. In medium bowl, stir together flour, sugar, cocoa, baking soda and salt. Add water, oil, vinegar and vanilla; beat with whisk just until batter is smooth and ingredients are well blended. Fill muffin cups ⅔ full with batter. Bake 16 to 18 minutes or until wooden pick inserted in center comes out clean. Remove from pans to wire racks. Cool completely. Frost as desired. *1½ dozen cupcakes*

Clockwise from top left: Quick Chocolate Cupcakes, Spicy Butterscotch Snack Cake (page 54), Apple Pie Chocolate Brownie Cake (page 54)

Spicy Butterscotch Snack Cake

1 cup (2 sticks) butter or
    margarine, softened
1 cup sugar
2 eggs
½ teaspoon vanilla extract
½ cup applesauce
2½ cups all-purpose flour
1½ to 2 teaspoons ground
    cinnamon

1 teaspoon baking soda
½ teaspoon salt
1⅔ cups (10-ounce package)
    HERSHEY'S Butterscotch
    Chips
1 cup chopped pecans
    (optional)
Powdered sugar (optional)

Heat oven to 350°F. Lightly grease 13×9×2-inch baking pan. In large mixer bowl, beat butter and sugar until light and fluffy. Add eggs and vanilla; beat well. Mix in applesauce. Stir together flour, cinnamon, baking soda and salt; gradually add to butter mixture, mixing well. Stir in butterscotch chips and pecans, if desired. Spread into prepared pan. Bake 35 to 40 minutes or until wooden pick inserted in center comes out clean. Cool completely in pan on wire rack. Sprinkle with powdered sugar, if desired. *12 servings*

Apple Pie Chocolate Brownie Cake

Apple Topping (recipe
    follows)
1 cup all-purpose flour
⅔ cup sugar
¼ cup HERSHEY'S Cocoa or
    HERSHEY'S European
    Style Cocoa
1 teaspoon baking powder

½ teaspoon salt
¾ cup water
⅔ cup shortening
1 egg
1 teaspoon vanilla extract
    Whipped topping *or* ice
    cream (optional)

Prepare Apple Topping. Heat oven to 375°F. Grease and flour 9-inch square baking pan. In medium bowl, stir together flour, sugar, cocoa, baking powder and salt. Add water, shortening, egg and vanilla; beat until smooth and well blended. Spread into prepared pan. Carefully spoon prepared topping over chocolate batter to within ½ inch of edges. *Do not stir*. Bake 35 to 40 minutes or until chocolate is set and cakelike. Cool completely in pan on wire rack. Serve with whipped topping, if desired. Garnish as desired.   *8 to 10 servings*

Apple Topping

1 can (20 ounces) apple pie filling

½ teaspoon lemon juice
½ teaspoon ground cinnamon

In small bowl, stir together apple pie filling, lemon juice and cinnamon.

Crunchy Topped Cocoa Cake

1½ cups all-purpose flour
1 cup sugar
¼ cup HERSHEY'S Cocoa
1 teaspoon baking soda
½ teaspoon salt
1 cup water

¼ cup plus 2 tablespoons vegetable oil
1 tablespoon white vinegar
1 teaspoon vanilla extract
Broiled Topping (recipe follows)

Heat oven to 350°F. Grease and flour 8-inch square baking pan. In large bowl, stir together flour, sugar, cocoa, baking soda and salt. Add water, oil, vinegar and vanilla; beat with spoon or whisk just until batter is smooth and ingredients are well blended. Pour batter into prepared pan. Bake 35 to 40 minutes or until wooden pick inserted in center comes out clean. Meanwhile, prepare Broiled Topping; spread onto warm cake. Preheat broiler; place cake about 4 inches from heat source. Broil 3 minutes or until topping is bubbly and golden brown. Remove from oven. Cool completely in pan on wire rack.   *9 servings*

Broiled Topping

¼ cup (½ stick) butter or margarine, softened
½ cup packed light brown sugar
½ cup coarsely chopped nuts

½ cup MOUNDS Sweetened Coconut Flakes
3 tablespoons light cream *or* evaporated milk

In small bowl, stir together butter, brown sugar, nuts, coconut and light cream until well blended.

Cherry Glazed Chocolate Torte

½ cup (1 stick) butter or
    margarine, melted
1 cup sugar
1 teaspoon vanilla extract
2 eggs
½ cup all-purpose flour

⅓ cup HERSHEY'S Cocoa
¼ teaspoon baking powder
¼ teaspoon salt
    Cream Layer (recipe follows)
1 can (21 ounces) cherry pie
    filling, divided

Heat oven to 350°F. Grease bottom of 9-inch springform pan. In large bowl, stir together butter, sugar and vanilla. Add eggs; using spoon, beat well. Stir together flour, cocoa, baking powder and salt; gradually add to egg mixture, beating until well blended. Spread batter into prepared pan. Bake 25 to 30 minutes or until cake is set. (Cake will be fudgey and will not test done.) Cool completely in pan on wire rack. Prepare Cream Layer; spread over top of cake. Spread 1 cup cherry pie filling over Cream Layer; refrigerate 3 hours. With knife, loosen cake from side of pan; remove side of pan. Serve with remaining pie filling. Garnish as desired. Cover; refrigerate leftover torte.   *10 to 12 servings*

Cream Layer

1 package (8 ounces) cream
    cheese, softened
1 cup powdered sugar

1 cup frozen non-dairy
    whipped topping, thawed

In small mixer bowl, beat cream cheese and powdered sugar until well blended. Fold in whipped topping.

Cherry Glazed Chocolate Torte

Hershey's Lavish Chocolate Cake

½ cup (1 stick) butter
1 cup sugar
1 cup milk
1 tablespoon white vinegar
½ teaspoon vanilla extract
1¼ cups all-purpose flour
⅓ cup HERSHEY'S Cocoa
1 teaspoon baking soda
　Dash salt

Chocolate Ganache (page 59)
Cocoa Mousse Filling (recipe
　follows)
2 to 4 tablespoons seedless
　black raspberry preserves
Sweetened whipped cream
Fresh raspberries (optional)
Additional HERSHEY'S
　Cocoa (optional)

Heat oven to 350°F. Line bottoms of three 8-inch round baking pans with wax paper. Lightly grease sides of pans. In large microwave-safe bowl, place butter. Microwave at HIGH (100%) 1 minute or until melted; stir in sugar. Add milk, vinegar and vanilla; stir until blended. Stir together flour, cocoa, baking soda and salt; gradually add to butter mixture, whisking until well blended. Pour batter evenly into prepared pans. Bake 15 minutes or until wooden pick inserted in center comes out clean. Cool 10 minutes. Remove from pans to wire racks; gently peel off wax paper. Cool completely. Prepare Chocolate Ganache and Cocoa Mousse Filling. Place one cake layer on serving plate; spread 1 to 2 tablespoons preserves over top. Carefully spread half of prepared filling over preserves. Refrigerate about 10 minutes. Place second layer on top; repeat procedure with remaining preserves and filling. Place remaining layer on top. Refrigerate about 10 minutes. Spread prepared ganache over top and sides of cake. Refrigerate at least 30 minutes. Just before serving, garnish with sweetened whipped cream and raspberries, if desired; sift additional cocoa over top, if desired. Refrigerate leftover cake.

12 servings

Cocoa Mousse Filling

1 teaspoon unflavored gelatin
1 tablespoon cold water
2 tablespoons boiling water
½ cup sugar

¼ cup HERSHEY'S Cocoa
1 cup (½ pint) cold whipping
　cream
1 teaspoon vanilla extract

In small bowl, sprinkle gelatin over cold water; let stand 2 minutes to soften. Add boiling water; stir until gelatin is completely dissolved and mixture is clear. Cool slightly. In small mixer bowl, stir together sugar and cocoa; add whipping cream and vanilla. Beat at medium speed of electric mixer, scraping bottom of bowl occasionally, until stiff; pour in gelatin mixture. Beat until well blended. Refrigerate about 20 minutes.

Chocolate Ganache

1 cup (½ pint) whipping cream

1½ cups HERSHEY'S Semi-Sweet Chocolate Chips

In small heavy saucepan over low heat, heat whipping cream until warm. Add chocolate chips; stir constantly, just until chips are melted and mixture is smooth. *Do not let mixture come to a boil.* Transfer mixture to medium bowl; refrigerate until of spreading consistency, about 1½ hours.

Quick Black Forest Cake

½ cup (1 stick) butter or margarine, softened
1 cup sugar
3 eggs
1 teaspoon vanilla extract
1 cup all-purpose flour
½ cup HERSHEY'S Cocoa
½ teaspoon baking soda

1 can (21 ounces) cherry pie filling
⅓ cup slivered almonds
½ teaspoon almond extract (optional)
Whipped cream or vanilla ice cream (optional)

Heat oven to 350°F. Lightly grease 13×9×2-inch baking pan. In large mixer bowl, beat butter and sugar until light and fluffy. Add eggs and vanilla; beat well. Stir together flour, cocoa and baking soda; gradually add to butter mixture, beating until well blended. Spoon batter into prepared pan. Stir together cherry pie filling, almonds and almond extract, if desired. Spoon cherry mixture over chocolate batter. Bake 45 to 50 minutes or until center of cake is firm. Serve warm or at room temperature with whipped cream or ice cream, if desired.

12 to 15 servings

Classic Boston Cream Pie

⅓ cup shortening
1 cup sugar
2 eggs
1 teaspoon vanilla extract
1¼ cups all-purpose flour

1½ teaspoons baking powder
¼ teaspoon salt
¾ cup milk
Rich Filling (recipe follows)
Dark Cocoa Glaze (page 62)

Heat oven to 350°F. Grease and flour 9-inch round baking pan. In large mixer bowl, beat shortening, sugar, eggs and vanilla until light and fluffy. Stir together flour, baking powder and salt; add alternately with milk to shortening mixture, beating well after each addition. Pour batter into prepared pan. Bake 30 to 35 minutes or until wooden pick inserted in center comes out clean. Cool 10 minutes; remove from pan to wire rack. Cool completely. Meanwhile, prepare Rich Filling. With long serrated knife, cut cake in half horizontally. Place one layer, cut side up, on serving plate; spread with prepared filling. Top with remaining layer, cut side down. Prepare Dark Cocoa Glaze; spread over cake, allowing glaze to run down sides. Refrigerate several hours or until cold. Garnish as desired. Refrigerate leftover pie.   *8 to 10 servings*

Rich Filling

⅓ cup sugar
2 tablespoons cornstarch
1½ cups milk
2 egg yolks, slightly beaten

1 tablespoon butter or
    margarine
1 teaspoon vanilla extract

In medium saucepan, stir together sugar and cornstarch; gradually add milk and egg yolks, stirring until blended. Cook over medium heat, stirring constantly, until mixture comes to a boil. Boil 1 minute, stirring constantly. Remove from heat; stir in butter and vanilla. Cover; refrigerate several hours or until cold.

continued on page 62

Classic Boston Cream Pie

Classic Boston Cream Pie (continued)

Dark Cocoa Glaze

3 tablespoons water
2 tablespoons butter or
   margarine
3 tablespoons HERSHEY'S
   Cocoa

1 cup powdered sugar
½ teaspoon vanilla extract

In small saucepan over medium heat, heat water and butter until mixture comes to a boil; remove from heat. Immediately stir in cocoa. Gradually add powdered sugar and vanilla, beating with whisk until smooth and of desired consistency; cool slightly.

Chocolate Truffle Cake Supreme

1¼ cups (2½ sticks) butter (do
   not use margarine)
¾ cup HERSHEY'S Cocoa
1 cup plus 1 tablespoon sugar,
   divided

1 tablespoon all-purpose flour
2 teaspoons vanilla extract
4 eggs, separated
1 cup (½ pint) cold whipping
   cream

Heat oven to 425°F. Grease bottom of 8-inch springform pan. In medium saucepan over low heat, melt butter. Add cocoa and 1 cup sugar; stir until well blended. Remove from heat; cool slightly. Stir in flour and vanilla. Add egg yolks, one at a time, beating well after each addition. In small mixer bowl on high speed of electric mixer, beat egg whites with remaining 1 tablespoon sugar until soft peaks form; gradually fold into chocolate mixture. Spread batter into prepared pan. Bake 16 to 18 minutes or until edge is firm. (Center will be soft.) Cool completely in pan on wire rack. (Cake will sink slightly in center as it cools.) Remove side of pan. Refrigerate cake at least 6 hours. In small mixer bowl on high speed, beat whipping cream until stiff; spread over top of cake. Cut cake while cold, but let stand at room temperature 10 to 15 minutes before serving.

10 servings

Grand Finale Cheesecake

Almond Graham Crust
(recipe follows)
1 SYMPHONY Milk Chocolate
Bar *or* Milk Chocolate Bar
With Almonds & Toffee
Chips (7 ounces), broken
into pieces
4 packages (3 ounces *each*)
cream cheese, softened

½ cup sugar
2 tablespoons HERSHEY'S
Cocoa
⅛ teaspoon salt
2 eggs
1 teaspoon vanilla extract
Whipped cream (optional)

Prepare Almond Graham Crust. Heat oven to 325°F. In small microwave-safe bowl, place chocolate. Microwave at HIGH (100%) 1 minute or until chocolate is melted and smooth when stirred. In large mixer bowl, beat cream cheese until smooth. Stir together sugar, cocoa and salt; blend into cream cheese mixture. Add eggs and vanilla; beat until well blended. Pour into prepared crust. Bake 35 to 40 minutes or until set in center. Remove from oven to wire rack. With knife, immediately loosen cake from side of pan. Cool completely; remove side of pan. Refrigerate several hours before serving. Garnish with whipped cream, if desired. Cover; refrigerate leftover cheesecake. *8 servings*

Almond Graham Crust

¾ cup graham cracker crumbs
⅔ cup finely chopped slivered
almonds

2 tablespoons sugar
¼ cup (½ stick) butter or
margarine, melted

In medium bowl, stir together crumbs, almonds and sugar. Stir in butter. Press mixture onto bottom and up side of 8-inch springform pan.

Top to bottom: Easy Rich No-Bake Chocolate Cheesecake (page 66), Butterscotch Cheesecake with Chocolate Drizzle (page 32), Chocolate Raspberry Cheesecake

Chocolate Raspberry Cheesecake

Chocolate Wafer Crust
(recipe follows)
1⅔ cups (10-ounce package)
HERSHEY'S Raspberry
Chips
2 packages (8 ounces *each*)
cream cheese, softened

¾ cup sugar
4 eggs
1 cup (8 ounces) sour cream
1 teaspoon vanilla extract
Sweetened whipped cream
Fresh raspberries (optional)

Prepare Chocolate Wafer Crust. Heat oven to 325°F. In medium microwave-safe bowl, place raspberry chips. Microwave at HIGH (100%) 1 minute; stir. If necessary, microwave at HIGH an additional 15 seconds at a time, stirring after each heating, just until chips are melted when stirred. In large mixer bowl on medium speed of electric mixer, beat cream cheese and sugar until smooth. Blend in melted chips. Add eggs, one at a time, beating well after each addition. Add sour cream and vanilla; blend well. Pour into prepared crust. Bake 55 to 60 minutes or until almost set in center. Remove from oven to wire rack. With knife, immediately loosen edge of cake from side of pan. Cool completely; remove side of pan. Cover; refrigerate several hours. Just before serving, garnish with sweetened whipped cream and raspberries, if desired. Refrigerate leftover cheesecake. *10 to 12 servings*

Chocolate Wafer Crust

6 tablespoons butter or
margarine
1½ cups vanilla wafer crumbs
(about 45 wafers)

6 tablespoons powdered sugar
6 tablespoons HERSHEY'S
Cocoa

In medium microwave-safe bowl, place butter. Microwave at HIGH (100%) 30 seconds or until melted. Stir in crumbs, powdered sugar and cocoa; blend well. Press mixture onto bottom and ½ inch up side of 9-inch springform pan.

Easy Rich No-Bake Chocolate Cheesecake

Almond Crumb Crust (recipe
   follows)
1 box (8 ounces) HERSHEY'S
   Semi-Sweet Baking
   Chocolate, broken into
   pieces
3 packages (3 ounces *each*)
   cream cheese, softened

¼ cup sugar
¼ cup (½ stick) butter or
   margarine, softened
1 teaspoon vanilla extract
1 cup (½ pint) cold whipping
   cream

Prepare Almond Crumb Crust. In small microwave-safe bowl, place chocolate. Microwave at HIGH (100%) 1½ to 2 minutes or until chocolate is melted when stirred. Cool slightly. In large mixer bowl on medium speed of electric mixer, beat cream cheese, sugar, butter and vanilla until smooth. On low speed, blend in melted chocolate. In small mixer bowl on high speed of electric mixer, beat whipping cream until stiff; fold into chocolate mixture. Pour into prepared crust. Cover; refrigerate several hours or until firm. Garnish as desired. Refrigerate leftover cheesecake.

8 servings

Almond Crumb Crust

1 cup finely chopped slivered
   almonds
¾ cup vanilla wafer crumbs

¼ cup powdered sugar
¼ cup (½ stick) butter or
   margarine, melted

Heat oven to 350°F. In medium bowl, stir together almonds, crumbs and powdered sugar; stir in butter. Press mixture onto bottom and halfway up side of 9-inch springform pan. Bake 8 to 10 minutes or until lightly browned. Cool completely.

No-Bake Cherry Chocolate Shortcake

1 frozen loaf pound cake
    (10¾ ounces), thawed
1 can (21 ounces) cherry pie
    filling, chilled
⅓ cup HERSHEY'S Cocoa or
    HERSHEY'S European
    Style Cocoa

½ cup powdered sugar
1 container (8 ounces) frozen
    non-dairy whipped
    topping, thawed (3½ cups)

Slice pound cake horizontally into three layers. Place bottom cake layer on serving plate; top with half the pie filling, using mostly cherries. Repeat with middle cake layer and remaining pie filling; place rounded layer on top. Cover; refrigerate several hours. Sift cocoa and powdered sugar onto whipped topping; stir until mixture is blended and smooth. Immediately spread over top and sides of cake, covering completely. Refrigerate leftover shortcake.　　*About 6 servings*

Quick & Easy Chocolate Cake

4 bars (1 ounce *each*)
    HERSHEY'S Unsweetened
    Baking Chocolate, broken
    into pieces
¼ cup (½ stick) butter or
    margarine
1⅔ cups boiling water

2⅓ cups all-purpose flour
2 cups sugar
½ cup dairy sour cream
2 eggs
2 teaspoons baking soda
1 teaspoon salt
1 teaspoon vanilla extract

Heat oven to 350°F. Grease and flour 13×9×2-inch baking pan. In large mixer bowl, combine chocolate, butter and water; with spoon, stir until chocolate is melted and mixture is smooth. Add flour, sugar, sour cream, eggs, baking soda, salt and vanilla; beat on low speed of electric mixer until smooth. Pour batter into prepared pan. Bake 35 to 40 minutes or until wooden pick inserted in center comes out clean. Cool completely in pan on wire rack. Frost as desired.

12 to 15 servings

Chocolate Orange Marble Chiffon Cake

⅓ cup HERSHEY'S Cocoa
¼ cup hot water
3 tablespoons plus 1½ cups
   sugar, divided
2 tablespoons plus ½ cup
   vegetable oil, divided
2¼ cups all-purpose flour
1 tablespoons baking powder

1 teaspoon salt
¾ cup cold water
7 egg yolks
1 cup egg whites (about 8)
½ teaspoon cream of tartar
1 tablespoon freshly grated
   orange peel
Orange Glaze (recipe follows)

Remove top oven rack; move other rack to lowest position. Heat oven to 325°F. In medium bowl, stir together cocoa and hot water. Stir in 3 tablespoons sugar and 2 tablespoons oil. In large bowl, stir together flour, remaining 1½ cups sugar, baking powder and salt. Add cold water, remaining ½ cup oil and egg yolks; beat with spoon until smooth. In large mixer bowl on high speed of electric mixer, beat egg whites and cream of tartar until stiff peaks form. Pour egg yolk mixture in a thin stream over egg white mixture, gently folding just until blended. Remove 2 cups batter; add to chocolate mixture, gently folding until well blended. Into remaining batter, fold orange peel. Spoon half the orange batter into ungreased 10-inch tube pan; drop half the chocolate batter on top by spoonfuls. Repeat layers of orange and chocolate batters. Gently swirl with knife for marbled effect, leaving definite orange and chocolate areas. Bake 1 hour and 15 to 20 minutes or until top springs back when touched lightly. Immediately invert cake onto heatproof funnel; cool cake completely. Remove cake from pan; invert onto serving plate. Prepare Orange Glaze; spread over top of cake, allowing glaze to run down sides. Garnish as desired. *12 to 16 servings*

Orange Glaze

⅓ cup butter or margarine
2 cups powdered sugar
2 tablespoons orange juice

½ teaspoon freshly grated
   orange peel

In medium saucepan over low heat, melt butter. Remove from heat; gradually stir in powdered sugar, orange juice and orange peel, beating until smooth and of desired consistency. Add additional orange juice, 1 teaspoon at a time, if needed.

Chocolate Orange Marble Chiffon Cake

Chocolate Rum Pecan Pound Cake

⅔ cup HERSHEY'S Cocoa, divided
¼ cup boiling water
1¼ cups (2½ sticks) butter or margarine, softened
2⅔ cups sugar
1 teaspoon vanilla extract
5 eggs
2 cups all-purpose flour
1 teaspoon salt

½ teaspoon baking powder
¼ teaspoon baking soda
½ cup buttermilk or sour milk*
¾ cup finely chopped pecans
¼ cup light rum *or* 1½ teaspoons rum extract plus ¼ cup water
Chocolate Chip Glaze (recipe follows)

*To sour milk: Use 1½ teaspoons white vinegar plus milk to equal ½ cup.

Heat oven to 325°F. Grease and flour 12-cup fluted tube pan. In small bowl, stir ⅓ cup cocoa and water until smooth; set aside. In large mixer bowl, beat butter, sugar and vanilla until light and fluffy. Add eggs, one at a time, beating well after each addition. Add reserved cocoa mixture; beat well. Stir together flour, remaining ⅓ cup cocoa, salt, baking powder and baking soda; add to butter mixture alternately with buttermilk, beating well after each addition. Stir in pecans and rum. Pour batter into prepared pan. Bake 1 hour 5 minutes or until wooden pick inserted in center comes out clean. Cool 10 minutes; remove from pan to wire rack. Cool completely. Prepare Chocolate Chip Glaze; drizzle over cake. *10 to 12 servings*

Chocolate Chip Glaze

3 tablespoons butter or margarine
3 tablespoons light corn syrup

1 tablespoon water
1 cup HERSHEY'S Semi-Sweet Chocolate Chips

In small saucepan, combine butter, corn syrup and water. Cook over medium heat, stirring constantly, until mixture comes to a boil. Remove from heat. Add chocolate chips; stir until melted. Cool slightly.

Chocolate Bar Filled Chocolate Cupcakes

Chocolate Bar Filling (recipe
  follows)
3 cups all-purpose flour
2 cups sugar
⅔ cup HERSHEY'S Cocoa
2 teaspoons baking soda
1 teaspoon salt

2 cups water
⅔ cup vegetable oil
2 tablespoons white vinegar
2 teaspoons vanilla extract
2 HERSHEY'S Milk Chocolate
  Bars (7 ounces *each*),
  broken into pieces

Prepare Chocolate Bar Filling. Heat oven to 350°F. Line muffin cups (2½ inches in diameter) with paper bake cups. In large mixer bowl, stir together flour, sugar, cocoa, baking soda and salt. Add water, oil, vinegar and vanilla; beat on medium speed of electric mixer 2 minutes. Fill muffin cups ⅔ full with batter. Spoon 1 level tablespoon prepared filling into center of each cupcake. Bake 20 to 25 minutes or until wooden pick inserted in cake portion comes out clean. Remove from pans to wire racks. Cool completely. Top each cupcake with chocolate bar piece.   *About 2½ dozen cupcakes*

Chocolate Bar Filling

1 package (8 ounces) cream
  cheese, softened
⅓ cup sugar
1 egg

⅛ teaspoon salt
1 HERSHEY'S Milk Chocolate
  Bar (7 ounces), cut into
  ¼-inch pieces

In small mixer bowl, beat cream cheese, sugar, egg and salt until smooth and creamy. Stir in chocolate bar pieces.

A Century of Excellence
1894 1994

COOKIE JAR FAVORITES

Chunky Macadamia Bars

¾ cup (1½ sticks) butter or
   margarine, softened
1 cup packed light brown
   sugar
½ cup granulated sugar
1 egg
1 teaspoon vanilla extract
2¼ cups all-purpose flour

1 teaspoon baking soda
1¾ cups (10-ounce package)
   HERSHEY'S Semi-Sweet
   Chocolate Chunks, divided
¾ cup coarsely chopped
   macadamia nuts
Quick Vanilla Glaze (recipe
   follows)

Heat oven to 375°F. In large mixer bowl, beat butter, brown sugar and granulated sugar until creamy. Add egg and vanilla; beat well. Add flour and baking soda; blend well. Stir in 1 cup chocolate chunks and nuts; press dough onto bottom of ungreased 13×9×2-inch baking pan. Sprinkle with remaining ¾ cup chocolate chunks. Bake 22 to 25 minutes or until golden brown. Cool completely in pan on wire rack. Prepare Quick Vanilla Glaze; drizzle over top of bars. Allow glaze to set. Cut into bars.   *About 24 bars*

Quick Vanilla Glaze

1 cup powdered sugar
2 tablespoons milk

½ teaspoon vanilla extract

In small bowl, combine powdered sugar, milk and vanilla; stir until smooth and of desired consistency.

Clockwise from top: Chunky Macadamia Bars, Chocolate Amaretto Squares (page 74),
Chocolate Pecan Pie Bars (page 74)

Chocolate Amaretto Squares

½ cup (1 stick) butter (do *not* use margarine), melted
1 cup sugar
2 eggs
½ cup all-purpose flour
⅓ cup HERSHEY'S Cocoa or HERSHEY'S European Style Cocoa

1¼ cups ground almonds
2 tablespoons almond-flavored liqueur *or* ½ teaspoon almond extract
Sliced almonds (optional)

Heat oven to 325°F. Grease 8-inch square baking pan. In large bowl, beat butter and sugar until creamy. Add eggs, flour and cocoa; beat well. Stir in ground almonds and almond liqueur. Pour batter into prepared pan. Bake 35 to 40 minutes or just until set. Cool completely in pan on wire rack. Cut into squares. Garnish with sliced almonds, if desired.   *About 16 squares*

Chocolate Pecan Pie Bars

1⅓ cups all-purpose flour
2 tablespoons plus ½ cup packed light brown sugar, divided
½ cup (1 stick) cold butter or margarine
2 eggs

½ cup light corn syrup
¼ cup HERSHEY'S Cocoa
2 tablespoons butter or margarine, melted
1 teaspoon vanilla extract
⅛ teaspoon salt
1 cup coarsely chopped pecans

Heat oven to 350°F. In large bowl, stir together flour and 2 tablespoons brown sugar. With pastry blender, cut in ½ cup butter until mixture resembles coarse crumbs; press onto bottom and about 1 inch up sides of ungreased 9-inch square baking pan. Bake 10 to 12 minutes or until set. Remove from oven. With back of spoon, lightly press crust into corners and against sides of pan. In small bowl, lightly beat eggs, corn syrup, remaining ½ cup brown sugar, cocoa, butter, vanilla and salt until well blended. Stir in pecans. Pour mixture over warm crust. Continue baking 25 minutes or until filling is set. Cool completely in pan on wire rack. Cut into bars.   *About 16 bars*

Coconut Brownie Bites

42 MOUNDS or ALMOND JOY
    Candy Bar Miniatures
½ cup (1 stick) butter or
    margarine, softened
½ cup packed light brown
    sugar
¼ cup granulated sugar

1 egg
1 teaspoon vanilla extract
1¼ cups all-purpose flour
⅓ cup HERSHEY'S Cocoa
¾ teaspoon baking soda
½ teaspoon salt

Remove wrappers from candies. Line small muffin cups (1¾ inches in diameter) with paper bake cups. In large mixer bowl, beat butter, brown sugar, granulated sugar, egg and vanilla until light and fluffy. Stir together flour, cocoa, baking soda and salt; gradually add to butter mixture, beating until well blended. Cover; refrigerate dough about 30 minutes or until firm enough to handle. Heat oven to 375°F. Shape dough into 1-inch balls; place one in each prepared muffin cup. *Do not flatten.* Bake 8 to 10 minutes or until puffed. Remove from oven. Cool 5 minutes. (Cookie will sink slightly.) Press one candy onto each cookie. Cool completely in pan on wire racks. *About 3½ dozen cookies*

Chocolatetown Chip Cookies

¾ cup (1½ sticks) butter (do
    not use margarine),
    softened
1 cup packed light brown
    sugar
½ cup granulated sugar
1 teaspoon vanilla extract

2 eggs
2 cups all-purpose flour
1 teaspoon baking soda
1 teaspoon salt
2 cups (12-ounce package)
    HERSHEY'S Semi-Sweet
    Chocolate Chips

Heat oven to 375°F. In large mixer bowl, beat butter, brown sugar, granulated sugar and vanilla until creamy. Add eggs; beat well. Stir together flour, baking soda and salt; gradually add to butter mixture, beating until blended. Stir in chocolate chips. Drop dough by teaspoonfuls onto ungreased cookie sheet. Bake 8 to 10 minutes or until lightly browned. Remove from cookie sheet to wire rack. Cool completely. *About 7 dozen cookies*

Giant Peanut Butter Cup Cookies

½ cup (1 stick) butter or
   margarine, softened
¾ cup sugar
⅓ cup REESE'S Creamy or
   Crunchy Peanut Butter
1 egg
½ teaspoon vanilla extract

1¼ cups all-purpose flour
½ teaspoon baking soda
¼ teaspoon salt
16 REESE'S Peanut Butter Cups
   Miniatures, cut into
   quarters

Heat oven to 350°F. In small mixer bowl, beat butter, sugar and peanut butter until creamy. Add egg and vanilla; beat well. Stir together flour, baking soda and salt. Add to butter mixture; blend well. Drop dough by level ¼-cup measurements onto ungreased cookie sheets, three cookies per sheet. (Cookies will spread while baking.) Press about 7 pieces of peanut butter cup into each cookie, flattening cookie slightly. Bake 15 to 17 minutes or until light golden brown around edges. Centers will be pale and slightly soft. Cool 1 minute on cookie sheet. Remove to wire rack; cool completely.
9 cookies

Chocolate Raspberry Brownies

1⅔ cups (10-ounce package)
   HERSHEY'S Raspberry
   Chips
¼ cup (½ stick) butter or
   margarine

2 eggs
1 teaspoon vanilla extract
1 cup all-purpose flour
½ cup sugar
1 teaspoon baking powder

Heat oven to 350°F. Grease 8-inch square baking pan. In medium saucepan, combine raspberry chips and butter. Cook over medium heat, stirring constantly, until melted. Remove from heat. Add eggs and vanilla; stir until well blended. Add flour, sugar and baking powder; stir until well blended. Spread batter into prepared pan. Bake 25 to 30 minutes or until brownies begin to pull away from sides of pan. Cool completely in pan on wire rack. Cut into squares.
About 20 brownies

Fudgey German Chocolate Sandwich Cookies

1¾ cups all-purpose flour
1½ cups sugar
¾ cup (1½ sticks) butter or
  margarine, softened
⅔ cup HERSHEY'S Cocoa or
  HERSHEY'S European
  Style Cocoa
¾ teaspoon baking soda

¼ teaspoon salt
2 eggs
2 tablespoons milk
1 teaspoon vanilla extract
½ cup finely chopped pecans
  Coconut and Pecan Filling
  (recipe follows)

Heat oven to 350°F. In large mixer bowl, combine flour, sugar, butter, cocoa, baking soda, salt, eggs, milk and vanilla. Beat at medium speed of electric mixer until blended. (Batter will be stiff.) Stir in pecans. Shape dough into 1¼-inch balls. Place on ungreased cookie sheet; flatten slightly. Bake 9 to 11 minutes or until almost set. Cool slightly; remove from cookie sheet to wire rack. Cool completely. Prepare Coconut and Pecan Filling. Spread flat side of one cookie with 1 heaping tablespoon prepared filling; cover with flat side of second cookie. Serve warm or at room temperature. *About 1½ dozen sandwich cookies*

Note: *Cookies can be reheated in microwave. Microwave at HIGH (100%) 10 seconds, or until filling is warm.*

Coconut and Pecan Filling

½ cup (1 stick) butter or
  margarine
½ cup packed light brown
  sugar
¼ cup light corn syrup

1 cup MOUNDS Sweetened
  Coconut Flakes, toasted*
1 cup finely chopped pecans
1 teaspoon vanilla extract

In medium saucepan over medium heat, melt butter. Add brown sugar and corn syrup; stir constantly until thick and bubbly. Remove from heat; stir in coconut, pecans and vanilla. Use warm.

*To toast coconut: Heat oven to 350°F. Spread coconut in even layer on baking sheet. Bake 6 to 8 minutes or until golden, stirring several times during toasting.

Clockwise from top left: Chocolate-Cherry Slice 'n' Bake Cookies, Peanut Butter Chip Oatmeal Cookies (page 81), Lemon Pecan Cookies (page 80)

Chocolate-Cherry Slice 'n' Bake Cookies

¾ cup (1½ sticks) butter or
    margarine, softened
1 cup sugar
1 egg
1½ teaspoons vanilla extract
2¼ cups all-purpose flour
2 teaspoons baking powder
½ teaspoon salt
¼ cup finely chopped
    maraschino cherries

½ teaspoon almond extract
    Red food color
⅓ cup HERSHEY'S Cocoa
¼ teaspoon baking soda
4 teaspoons water
    Cocoa Almond Glaze (recipe
    follows)

In large mixer bowl, beat butter, sugar, egg and vanilla until light and fluffy. Stir together flour, baking powder and salt; gradually add to butter mixture, beating until mixture forms a smooth dough. Remove 1¼ cups dough to medium bowl; blend in cherries, almond extract and about 6 drops food color. Stir together cocoa and baking soda. Add with water to remaining dough; blend until smooth. Divide chocolate dough in half; roll each half between two sheets of wax paper, forming 12×4½-inch rectangle. Remove top sheet of wax paper. Divide cherry mixture in half; with floured hands, shape each half into 12-inch roll. Place one roll in center of each rectangle; wrap chocolate dough around roll, forming one large roll. Wrap in plastic wrap. Refrigerate about 6 hours or until firm. Heat oven to 350°F. Cut rolls into ¼-inch-thick slices; place on ungreased cookie sheet. Bake 7 minutes or until set. Cool 1 minute; remove from cookie sheet to wire rack. Cool completely. Prepare Cocoa Almond Glaze; decorate cookies. *About 7½ dozen cookies*

Cocoa Almond Glaze

2 tablespoons butter or
    margarine
2 tablespoons HERSHEY'S
    Cocoa

2 tablespoons water
1 cup powdered sugar
⅛ teaspoon almond extract

In small saucepan over low heat, melt butter. Add cocoa and water; stir constantly until mixture thickens. *Do not boil.* Remove from heat. Add sugar and almond extract, beating until smooth and of desired consistency.

Lemon Pecan Cookies

1⅔ cups (10-ounce package)
   HERSHEY'S Vanilla Milk
   Chips, divided
2¼ cups all-purpose flour
¾ cup sugar
2 eggs
¾ teaspoon baking soda
½ teaspoon freshly grated
   lemon peel

¼ teaspoon lemon extract
½ cup (1 stick) butter or
   margarine
¾ cup chopped pecans
   Lemon Drizzle (recipe
   follows)

Heat oven to 350°F. Reserve 2 tablespoons vanilla milk chips for drizzle. In large mixer bowl, place flour, sugar, eggs, baking soda, lemon peel and lemon extract. In medium microwave-safe bowl, place remaining vanilla milk chips and butter. Microwave at HIGH (100%) 1 minute; stir. If necessary, microwave at HIGH an additional 15 seconds at a time, stirring after each heating, just until chips and butter are melted when stirred. Add vanilla chip mixture to flour mixture; beat until blended. Stir in pecans. Drop dough by rounded teaspoonfuls onto ungreased cookie sheet. Bake 9 to 11 minutes or until very slightly golden around edges. Remove from cookie sheet to wire rack. Cool completely. Prepare Lemon Drizzle; lightly drizzle over cookies.   *About 3½ dozen cookies*

Lemon Drizzle

2 tablespoons HERSHEY'S
   Vanilla Milk Chips
   (reserved from cookies)
½ teaspoon shortening (do
   not use butter, margarine
   or oil)

Yellow food color
Lemon extract

In small microwave-safe bowl, place reserved vanilla milk chips and shortening. Microwave at HIGH (100%) 30 seconds; stir. If necessary, microwave at HIGH an additional 15 seconds at a time, stirring after each heating, just until chips are melted when stirred. Stir in a few drops food color and a few drops lemon extract, if desired.

Peanut Butter Chip Oatmeal Cookies

1 cup (2 sticks) butter or
  margarine, softened
¼ cup shortening
2 cups packed light brown
  sugar
1 tablespoon milk
2 teaspoons vanilla extract
1 egg
2 cups all-purpose flour

1⅔ cups (10-ounce package)
  REESE'S Peanut Butter
  Chips
1½ cups quick-cooking or
  regular rolled oats
½ cup chopped walnuts
½ teaspoon baking soda
½ teaspoon salt

Heat oven to 375°F. In large mixer bowl, beat butter, shortening, brown sugar, milk, vanilla and egg until light and fluffy. Add remaining ingredients; mix until well blended. Drop dough by rounded teaspoonfuls about 2 inches apart onto ungreased cookie sheet. Bake until light brown, 10 to 12 minutes for soft cookies or 12 to 14 minutes for crisp cookies. Remove from cookie sheet to wire rack. Cool completely. *About 6 dozen cookies*

Chocolate Syrup Brownies

1 egg
1 cup packed light brown
  sugar
¾ cup HERSHEY'S Syrup
1½ cups all-purpose flour
¼ teaspoon baking soda

Dash salt
½ cup (1 stick) butter (do *not*
  use margarine), melted
¾ cup chopped pecans or
  walnuts

Heat oven to 350°F. Grease 9-inch square baking pan. In small mixer bowl, beat egg lightly; add brown sugar and syrup, beating until well blended. Stir together flour, baking soda and salt; gradually add to egg mixture, beating until blended. Stir in butter and nuts. Spread batter into prepared pan. Bake 35 to 40 minutes or until brownies begin to pull away from sides of pan. Cool completely in pan on wire rack. Cut into squares. *About 16 brownies*

Three-In-One Chocolate Chip Cookies

6 tablespoons butter or
    margarine, softened
½ cup packed light brown
    sugar
¼ cup granulated sugar
1 egg
1 teaspoon vanilla extract
1½ cups all-purpose flour

½ teaspoon baking soda
¼ teaspoon salt
2 cups (12-ounce package)
    HERSHEY'S Semi-Sweet
    Chocolate Chips *or* 1¾
    cups (10-ounce package)
    HERSHEY'S Semi-Sweet
    Chocolate Chunks

In large mixer bowl, beat butter, brown sugar and granulated sugar until creamy. Add egg and vanilla; beat well. Stir together flour, baking soda and salt; gradually add to butter mixture, blending well. Stir in chocolate chips. Shape and bake cookies into one of the three versions below:

Giant Three-In-One Chocolate Chip Cookie: *Prepare dough as directed. Heat oven to 350°F. Line 12×⅝-inch pizza pan with foil. Pat dough into prepared pan to within ¾ inch of edge. Bake 15 to 18 minutes or until lightly browned. Cool completely; cut into wedges. Makes 8 servings.*

Medium-Size Three-In-One Chocolate Chip Refrigerator Cookies: *Prepare dough with semi-sweet chocolate chips. On wax paper, shape dough into two rolls, each 1½ inches in diameter. Wrap in wax paper; cover tightly with plastic wrap. Refrigerate several hours or until firm enough to slice. Heat oven to 350°F. Remove rolls from refrigerator; remove wrapping. With sharp knife, cut into ¼-inch-thick slices. Place about 3 inches apart on ungreased cookie sheet. Bake 8 to 10 minutes or until lightly browned. Cool slightly; remove from cookie sheet to wire rack. Cool completely. Makes about 2½ dozen (2½-inch) cookies.*

Miniature Three-In-One Chocolate Chip Cookies: *Prepare dough with semi-sweet chocolate chips. Heat oven to 350°F. Drop dough by ¼ teaspoonfuls, about 1½ inches apart, onto ungreased cookie sheet. (Or, spoon dough into disposable plastic frosting bag; cut about ¼ inch off tip. Squeeze batter by ¼ teaspoonfuls onto ungreased cookie sheet.) Bake 5 to 7 minutes or just until set. Cool slightly; remove from cookie sheet to wire rack. Cool completely. Makes about 18 dozen (¾-inch) cookies.*

Giant Three-In-One Chocolate Chip Cookie

Symphony Milk Chocolate Macadamia Cookies

1 SYMPHONY Milk Chocolate Bar or Milk Chocolate Bar with Almonds & Toffee Chips (7 ounces)
6 tablespoons butter or margarine, softened
½ cup granulated sugar
¼ cup packed light brown sugar
½ teaspoon vanilla extract
1 egg
1 cup all-purpose flour
½ teaspoon baking soda
1 cup coarsely chopped macadamia nuts

Heat oven to 350°F. Cut chocolate bar into ¼-inch pieces. In large mixer bowl, beat butter, granulated sugar, brown sugar and vanilla until creamy. Add egg; beat well. Stir together flour and baking soda. Add to butter mixture; blend well. Stir in macadamia nuts and chocolate pieces. Drop dough by heaping tablespoonfuls onto ungreased cookie sheet. Bake 10 to 12 minutes or until lightly browned. Cool slightly; remove from cookie sheet to wire rack. Cool completely.

About 2 dozen cookies

Doubly Chocolate Mint Cookies

1 HERSHEY'S Cookies 'n' Mint Milk Chocolate Bar (7 ounces)
½ cup (1 stick) butter or margarine, softened
¾ cup sugar
1 egg
1 teaspoon vanilla extract
1 cup all-purpose flour
⅓ cup HERSHEY'S Cocoa
½ teaspoon baking soda
⅛ teaspoon salt
1 cup coarsely chopped nuts (optional)

Heat oven to 350°F. Cut chocolate bar into small pieces. In large mixer bowl, beat butter, sugar, egg and vanilla until light and fluffy. Stir together flour, cocoa, baking soda and salt. Blend into butter mixture. Stir in chocolate pieces and nuts, if desired. Drop dough by rounded teaspoonfuls onto ungreased cookie sheet. Bake 10 to 12 minutes or until set. Cool slightly; remove from cookie sheet to wire rack. Cool completely.

About 2½ dozen cookies

Cocoa Ginger Crisps

1 cup (2 sticks) butter or
   margarine, softened
1⅓ cups sugar, divided
1 egg
¼ cup light corn syrup
2 cups all-purpose flour

6 tablespoons plus 1¼
   teaspoons HERSHEY'S
   Cocoa, divided
2 teaspoons baking soda
¼ teaspoon ground ginger
¼ teaspoon salt

In large mixer bowl, beat butter, 1 cup sugar and egg until light and fluffy. Add corn syrup; beat until well blended. Stir together flour, 6 tablespoons cocoa, baking soda, ginger and salt; gradually add to butter mixture, beating until well blended. Cover; refrigerate dough about 1 hour or until firm enough to handle. Heat oven to 350°F. In shallow bowl, stir together remaining ⅓ cup sugar and 1¼ teaspoons cocoa. Shape dough into 1-inch balls; roll in sugar-cocoa mixture to coat. Place about 2 inches apart on ungreased cookie sheet. Bake 10 to 12 minutes or until cookies flatten. Cool 1 minute; remove from cookie sheet to wire rack. Cool completely. *About 4 dozen cookies*

Chewy Toffee Almond Bars

1 cup (2 sticks) butter (do *not*
   use margarine), softened
½ cup sugar
2 cups all-purpose flour
1¾ cups (10-ounce package)
   SKOR English Toffee Bits

¾ cup light corn syrup
1 cup sliced almonds, divided
¾ cup MOUNDS Sweetened
   Coconut Flakes, divided

Heat oven to 350°F. Grease sides of 13×9×2-inch baking pan. In large mixer bowl, beat butter and sugar until creamy. Gradually add flour, beating until well blended. Press dough into prepared pan. Bake 15 to 20 minutes or until edges are lightly browned. Meanwhile, in medium saucepan, stir together toffee bits and corn syrup. Cook over medium heat, stirring constantly, until toffee is melted, about 12 minutes. Stir in ½ cup almonds and ½ cup coconut. Spread toffee mixture to within ¼ inch of edges of crust. Sprinkle remaining ½ cup almonds and remaining ¼ cup coconut over top. Continue baking 15 minutes or until bubbly. Cool completely in pan on wire rack. Cut into bars. *About 36 bars*

Left to right: Dusted Cocoa-Cinnamon Cookies, Cocoa Pecan Crescents

Dusted Cocoa-Cinnamon Cookies

1 cup (2 sticks) butter or
  margarine, softened
⅔ cup granulated sugar
2 teaspoons milk
2 teaspoons vanilla extract
1⅔ cups all-purpose flour

⅓ cup HERSHEY'S Cocoa
1 cup finely chopped toasted
  almonds*
1 cup powdered sugar
1 tablespoon ground cinnamon

To toast almonds: Heat oven to 350°F. Spread almonds in even layer in shallow baking pan. Bake 8 to 10 minutes or until light golden brown, stirring occasionally; cool.

In large mixer bowl, beat butter and granulated sugar until creamy. Add milk and vanilla; beat well. Stir together flour and cocoa; gradually add to butter mixture, beating until well blended. Stir in almonds. Cover; refrigerate dough 1 hour or until firm enough to handle. Heat oven to 350°F. Shape dough into finger shapes, each 3 inches long and ½ inch wide. Place on ungreased cookie sheet. Bake 20 minutes or until set; remove from cookie sheet to wire rack. Cool slightly. In small bowl, stir together powdered sugar and cinnamon. Roll warm cookies in powdered sugar mixture. Cool completely.   *About 2½ dozen cookies*

Cocoa Pecan Crescents

1 cup (2 sticks) butter or
  margarine, softened
⅔ cup granulated sugar
1½ teaspoons vanilla extract
1¾ cups all-purpose flour

⅓ cup HERSHEY'S Cocoa
⅛ teaspoon salt
1½ cups ground pecans
  Powdered sugar

In large mixer bowl, beat butter, granulated sugar and vanilla until light and fluffy. Stir together flour, cocoa and salt; gradually add to butter mixture, blending well. Stir in pecans. Cover; refrigerate dough about 1 hour or until firm. Heat oven to 375°F. Shape scant tablespoonfuls of dough into logs about 2½ inches long; place on ungreased cookie sheet. Shape logs into crescents, tapering ends. Bake 13 to 15 minutes or until set. Cool slightly; remove from cookie sheet to wire rack. Cool completely. Roll in powdered sugar.   *About 3½ dozen cookies*

Chocolate Brownies Deluxe

½ cup (1 stick) butter or
   margarine, softened
1 cup sugar
2 eggs
1 teaspoon vanilla extract
1¼ cups all-purpose flour
¼ cup HERSHEY'S Cocoa

¼ teaspoon baking soda
¾ cup HERSHEY'S Syrup
1 cup REESE'S Peanut Butter
   Chips (optional)
Fudge Brownie Frosting
   (recipe follows)

Heat oven to 350°F. Grease 13×9×2-inch baking pan. In large mixer bowl, beat butter, sugar, eggs and vanilla until light and fluffy. Stir together flour, cocoa and baking soda; add alternately with syrup to butter mixture, beating well after each addition. Stir in peanut butter chips, if desired. Spread batter into prepared pan. Bake 40 to 45 minutes or until brownies begin to pull away from sides of pan. Cool completely in pan on wire rack. Prepare Fudge Brownie Frosting; spread over brownies. Cut into bars.
About 24 brownies

Fudge Brownie Frosting

3 tablespoons butter or
   margarine, softened
3 tablespoons HERSHEY'S
   Cocoa

1 cup powdered sugar
1 tablespoon milk
¾ teaspoon vanilla extract

In small mixer bowl, beat butter and cocoa until well blended; gradually add powdered sugar alternately with combined milk and vanilla, beating until smooth and of spreading consistency. Add additional milk, ½ teaspoon at a time, if needed.

Championship Chocolate Chip Bars

1½ cups all-purpose flour
½ cup packed light brown
   sugar
½ cup (1 stick) cold butter or
   margarine
2 cups (12-ounce package)
   HERSHEY'S Semi-Sweet
   Chocolate Chips, divided

1 can (14 ounces) sweetened
   condensed milk (*not*
   evaporated milk)
1 egg
1 teaspoon vanilla extract
1 cup chopped nuts

Heat oven to 350°F. In medium bowl, stir together flour and brown sugar; with pastry blender, cut in butter until mixture resembles coarse crumbs. Stir in ½ cup chocolate chips; press mixture onto bottom of 13×9×2-inch baking pan. Bake 15 minutes. Meanwhile, in large bowl, combine sweetened condensed milk, egg and vanilla. Stir in remaining 1½ cups chips and nuts. Spread over baked crust. Continue baking 25 minutes or until golden brown. Cool completely in pan on wire rack. Cut into bars. *About 36 bars*

Deep Dark Chocolate Cookies

¾ cup (1½ sticks) butter or
   margarine, softened
¾ cup granulated sugar
½ cup packed light brown
   sugar
1 teaspoon vanilla extract
2 eggs
1¾ cups all-purpose flour

½ cup HERSHEY'S Cocoa
¾ teaspoon baking soda
½ teaspoon baking powder
¼ teaspoon salt
1 cup HERSHEY'S Semi-Sweet
   Chocolate Chips
½ cup chopped nuts

Heat oven to 375°F. In large mixer bowl on medium speed of electric mixer, beat butter, granulated sugar, brown sugar and vanilla 2 minutes or until light and fluffy. Add eggs; beat well. Stir together flour, cocoa, baking soda, baking powder and salt; gradually add to butter mixture, beating just until blended. Stir in chocolate chips and nuts. Drop dough by heaping teaspoonfuls onto ungreased cookie sheet. Bake 7 minutes or until set. Cool 1 minute; remove from cookie sheet to wire rack. Cool completely. *About 4 dozen cookies*

Butterscotch Chewy Cookies

¾ cup (1½ sticks) butter or
   margarine, softened
1 cup packed light brown
   sugar
¼ cup light corn syrup
1 egg
1⅔ cups (10-ounce package)
   HERSHEY'S Butterscotch
   Chips, divided

2½ cups all-purpose flour
2 teaspoons baking soda
¼ teaspoon salt
1 to 1¼ cups finely ground
   nuts
Butterscotch Chip Drizzle
   (recipe follows)

In large mixer bowl, beat butter and brown sugar until creamy. Add corn syrup and egg; blend well. Reserve ⅔ cup butterscotch chips for glaze. In small microwave-safe bowl, microwave remaining 1 cup butterscotch chips at HIGH (100%) 1 minute; stir. If necessary, microwave at HIGH an additional 15 seconds at a time, stirring after each heating, just until chips are melted when stirred. Blend into butter mixture. Stir together flour, baking soda and salt; gradually add to butterscotch mixture, blending well. Refrigerate 1 hour or until dough is firm enough to handle. Heat oven to 350°F. Shape dough into 1-inch balls; roll in nuts, lightly pressing nuts into dough. Place on ungreased cookie sheet. Bake 8 to 10 minutes or until golden around edges. Cool several minutes; remove from cookie sheet to wire rack. Cool completely. Prepare Butterscotch Chip Drizzle; drizzle over cookies.
About 5 dozen cookies

Butterscotch Chip Drizzle

⅔ cup HERSHEY'S
   Butterscotch Chips
   (reserved from cookies)

1½ teaspoons shortening (do
   not use butter, margarine
   or oil)

In small microwave-safe bowl, place reserved butterscotch chips and shortening. Microwave at HIGH (100%) 1 minute; stir. If necessary, microwave at HIGH an additional 15 seconds at a time, stirring after each heating, just until chips are melted when stirred.

Oatmeal Brownie Drops

½ cup (1 stick) butter or
   margarine, softened
¾ cup sugar
2 eggs
1 teaspoon vanilla extract
1 cup all-purpose flour

½ cup HERSHEY'S Cocoa
¼ teaspoon baking soda
1 cup quick-cooking rolled oats
1 cup HERSHEY'S MINI
   CHIPS Semi-Sweet
   Chocolate

Heat oven to 350°F. In large mixer bowl, beat together butter and sugar until creamy. Add eggs and vanilla; beat well. Stir together flour, cocoa and baking soda; gradually add to butter mixture, blending thoroughly. Stir in oats and small chocolate chips. Drop dough by tablespoonfuls onto ungreased cookie sheet. Bake 7 to 8 minutes or until cookie begins to set. *Do not overbake.* Remove from cookie sheet to wire rack. Cool completely. *About 3½ dozen cookies*

Peanut Butter Chip and Walnut Squares

1 cup (2 sticks) butter or
   margarine, softened
1 cup packed light brown
   sugar
1 egg
1 teaspoon vanilla extract
2 cups all-purpose flour

½ cup light corn syrup
6 tablespoons butter or
   margarine
1⅔ cups (10-ounce package)
   REESE'S Peanut Butter
   Chips
¾ cup chopped walnuts

Heat oven to 350°F. In large mixer bowl, beat 1 cup butter, brown sugar, egg and vanilla until light and fluffy. Stir in flour. Spread batter into ungreased 13×9×2-inch baking pan. Bake 20 to 22 minutes or until lightly browned. Cool completely in pan on wire rack. In medium saucepan over low heat, cook corn syrup, 6 tablespoons butter and peanut butter chips, stirring constantly until chips are melted. Working quickly, spread mixture over baked layer. Sprinkle with walnuts; gently press into mixture. Refrigerate, uncovered, about 2 hours or until firm. Cut into squares. *About 36 squares*

Brownie Caramel Pecan Bars

½ cup sugar
2 tablespoons butter or
　margarine
2 tablespoons water
2 cups (12-ounce package)
　HERSHEY'S Semi-Sweet
　Chocolate Chips, divided
2 eggs

1 teaspoon vanilla extract
⅔ cup all-purpose flour
¼ teaspoon baking soda
¼ teaspoon salt
　Caramel Topping (recipe
　follows)
1 cup pecan pieces

Heat oven to 350°F. Line 9-inch square baking pan with foil, extending foil over edges of pan. Grease and flour foil. In medium saucepan, combine sugar, butter and water; cook over low heat, stirring constantly, until mixture comes to a boil. Remove from heat. Immediately add 1 cup chocolate chips; stir until melted. Beat in eggs and vanilla until well blended. Stir together flour, baking soda and salt; stir into chocolate mixture. Spread into prepared pan. Bake 15 to 20 minutes or until brownies begin to pull away from sides of pan. Meanwhile, prepare Caramel Topping. Remove brownies from oven; immediately and carefully spread with prepared topping. Sprinkle remaining 1 cup chips and pecans over topping. Cool completely in pan on wire rack, being careful not to disturb chips while still soft. Use foil to lift brownies out of pan; peel off foil. Cut into bars.　　*About 16 bars*

Caramel Topping

25 caramels
¼ cup (½ stick) butter or
　margarine

2 tablespoons milk

Remove wrappers from caramels. In medium microwave-safe bowl, place caramels, butter and milk. Microwave at HIGH (100%) 1 minute; stir. Microwave an additional 1 to 2 minutes, stirring every 30 seconds, or until caramels are melted and mixture is smooth when stirred. Use immediately.

Clockwise from top left: Brownie Caramel Pecan Bars, Raspberry Vanilla Nut Bars (page 94), Chewy Rocky Road Bars (page 94), Championship Chocolate Chip Bars (page 89)

Chewy Rocky Road Bars

1½ cups finely crushed unsalted
    pretzels
¾ cup (1½ sticks) butter or
    margarine, melted
1 can (14 ounces) sweetened
    condensed milk (*not*
    evaporated milk)
2 cups miniature
    marshmallows

1 cup HERSHEY'S
    Butterscotch Chips
1 cup HERSHEY'S Semi-Sweet
    Chocolate Chips
1 cup MOUNDS Sweetened
    Coconut Flakes
¾ cup chopped nuts

Heat oven to 350°F. In small bowl, combine pretzels and butter; spread mixture onto bottom of ungreased 13×9×2-inch baking pan. Pour sweetened condensed milk over crumb mixture, spreading to edges of pan. Top with marshmallows, butterscotch chips, chocolate chips, coconut and nuts. Press toppings firmly into sweetened condensed milk. Bake 25 to 30 minutes or until lightly browned. Cool completely in pan on wire rack. Cut into bars. *About 36 bars*

Note: *2 cups (12-ounce package) HERSHEY'S Semi-Sweet Chocolate Chips or 1⅔ cups (10-ounce package) HERSHEY'S Butterscotch Chips may be used instead of 1 cup each flavor.*

Raspberry Vanilla Nut Bars

1⅔ cups (10-ounce package)
    HERSHEY'S Vanilla Milk
    Chips, divided
¾ cup (1½ sticks) butter or
    margarine
2¼ cups all-purpose flour
¾ cup sugar
3 eggs

¾ teaspoon baking powder
1⅔ cups (10-ounce package)
    HERSHEY'S Raspberry
    Chips, divided
½ cup chopped pecans
    Double Drizzle

Heat oven to 350°F. Grease 13×9×2-inch baking pan. Reserve 2 tablespoons vanilla milk chips for drizzle. In medium microwave-safe bowl, combine remaining vanilla milk chips and butter. Microwave at HIGH (100%) 1½ minutes; stir. If necessary, microwave an additional 15 seconds at a time, stirring after each heating, just until chips are melted when stirred. In large mixer bowl, combine flour, sugar, eggs and baking powder. Add vanilla milk chip mixture; beat well. Reserve 2 tablespoons raspberry chips for drizzle. Chop remaining raspberry chips in food processor (use pulsing motion); stir into batter with pecans. Spread into prepared pan. Bake 25 minutes or until edges pull away from sides of pan and top surface is golden. Cool completely in pan on wire rack. Prepare Double Drizzle; using one flavor at a time, drizzle over bars. Cut into bars.

About 24 bars

Double Drizzle

2 tablespoons HERSHEY'S
    Vanilla Milk Chips
    (reserved from bars)
1 teaspoon shortening (do
    not use butter, margarine
    or oil), divided

2 tablespoons HERSHEY'S
    Raspberry Chips (reserved
    from bars)

In small microwave-safe bowl, place vanilla milk chips and ½ teaspoon shortening. Microwave at HIGH (100%) 30 seconds; stir. If necessary, microwave at HIGH an additional 15 seconds at a time, stirring after each heating, just until chips are melted when stirred. Repeat procedure with raspberry chips and remaining ½ teaspoon shortening.

Peanut Butter and Chocolate Bars: *Omit HERSHEY'S Vanilla Milk Chips; replace with 1⅔ cups REESE'S Peanut Butter Chips. Omit HERSHEY'S Raspberry Chips; replace with 1⅔ cups HERSHEY'S Semi-Sweet Chocolate Chips. Omit chopped pecans; replace with chopped peanuts.*

Butterscotch and Chocolate Bars: *Omit HERSHEY'S Vanilla Milk Chips; replace with 1⅔ cups HERSHEY'S Butterscotch Chips. Omit HERSHEY'S Raspberry Chips; replace with 1⅔ cups HERSHEY'S Semi-Sweet Chocolate Chips. Omit chopped pecans; replace with chopped walnuts.*

Quick & Easy Fudgey Brownies

4 bars (1 ounce *each*)
   HERSHEY'S Unsweetened
   Baking Chocolate, broken
   into pieces
¾ cup (1½ sticks) butter or
   margarine
2 cups sugar

3 eggs
1½ teaspoons vanilla extract
1 cup all-purpose flour
1 cup chopped nuts (optional)
   Quick & Easy Chocolate
   Frosting (recipe follows,
   optional)

Heat oven to 350°F. Grease 13×9×2-inch baking pan. In large microwave-safe bowl, place chocolate and butter. Microwave at HIGH (100%) 1½ to 2 minutes or until chocolate is melted and mixture is smooth when stirred. Add sugar; stir with spoon until well blended. Add eggs and vanilla; mix well. Stir in flour and nuts, if desired; stir until well blended. Spread into prepared pan. Bake 30 to 35 minutes or until wooden pick inserted in center comes out almost clean. Cool completely in pan on wire rack. Prepare Quick & Easy Chocolate Frosting, if desired. Spread over brownies. Cut into squares. *About 24 brownies*

Quick & Easy Chocolate Frosting

3 bars (1 ounce *each*)
   HERSHEY'S Unsweetened
   Baking Chocolate, broken
   into pieces
1 cup miniature marshmallows

½ cup (1 stick) butter or
   margarine, softened
⅓ cup milk
2½ cups powdered sugar
½ teaspoon vanilla extract

In medium, heavy saucepan over low heat, melt chocolate, stirring constantly. Add marshmallows; stir frequently until melted. (Mixture will be very thick and will pull away from sides of pan.) Spoon mixture into small mixer bowl. Add butter; beat well. Gradually add milk, beating until blended. Add powdered sugar and vanilla; beat until smooth and of spreading consistency. Add additional milk, 1 teaspoon at a time, if needed.

Quick & Easy Fudgey Brownies

Brownies with Peanut Butter Chips

1¼ cups (2½ sticks) butter or
   margarine, melted
1¾ cups sugar
4 eggs
2 teaspoons vanilla extract
1⅔ cups all-purpose flour
⅔ cup HERSHEY'S Cocoa

½ teaspoon baking powder
½ teaspoon salt
1⅔ cups (10-ounce package)
   REESE'S Peanut Butter
   Chips, divided
Peanut Butter Chip Glaze
   (recipe follows)

Heat oven to 350°F. Grease 13×9×2-inch baking pan. In large bowl, stir together butter and sugar. Add eggs and vanilla; beat with spoon or whisk until well blended. Stir together flour, cocoa, baking powder and salt; gradually add to butter mixture, stirring until well blended. Reserve ½ cup peanut butter chips for glaze; stir remaining chips into batter. Spread batter into prepared pan. Bake 30 to 35 minutes or until wooden pick inserted in center comes out clean. Cool completely in pan on wire rack. Prepare Peanut Butter Chip Glaze; drizzle over brownies. Let stand until glaze is set. Cut into squares.   *About 32 brownies*

Peanut Butter Chip Glaze

½ cup REESE'S Peanut Butter
   Chips (reserved from
   brownies)
2 tablespoons butter or
   margarine

2 tablespoons milk
¼ cup powdered sugar

In small microwave-safe bowl, place peanut butter chips, butter and milk. Microwave at HIGH (100%) 45 seconds; stir. If necessary, microwave at HIGH an additional 15 seconds at a time, stirring after each heating, just until chips are melted when stirred. Add powdered sugar; beat with whisk until smooth.

***Top to bottom: Sensational Peppermint Pattie Brownies (page 100), Brownies with Peanut
Butter Chips, Chocolate Cream Cheese Brownies (page 100)***

Sensational Peppermint Pattie Brownies

24 small (1½-inch) YORK
    Peppermint Patties
1½ cups (3 sticks) butter or
    margarine, melted
3 cups sugar
1 tablespoon vanilla extract

5 eggs
2 cups all-purpose flour
1 cup HERSHEY'S Cocoa
1 teaspoon baking powder
1 teaspoon salt

Heat oven to 350°F. Remove wrappers from peppermint patties. Grease 13×9×2-inch baking pan. In large bowl with spoon or whisk, stir together butter, sugar and vanilla. Add eggs; stir until well blended. Stir together flour, cocoa, baking powder and salt; gradually add to butter mixture, blending well. Reserve 2 cups batter. Spread remaining batter into prepared pan. Arrange peppermint patties about ½ inch apart in single layer over batter. Spread reserved batter over patties. Bake 50 to 55 minutes or until brownies begin to pull away from sides of pan. Cool completely in pan on wire rack. Cut into squares. *About 3 dozen brownies*

Chocolate Cream Cheese Brownies

1 cup (2 sticks) butter or
    margarine, softened
1 package (3 ounces) cream
    cheese, softened
2 cups sugar
3 eggs
1 teaspoon vanilla extract

1 cup all-purpose flour
¾ cup HERSHEY'S Cocoa
¼ teaspoon baking powder
½ teaspoon salt
¾ cup chopped nuts
    Brownie Frosting (recipe
    follows)

Heat oven to 325°F. Grease bottom of 13×9×2-inch baking pan. In large mixer bowl, beat butter, cream cheese and sugar until light and fluffy. Add eggs and vanilla; beat well. Stir together flour, cocoa, baking powder and salt; gradually add to butter mixture, blending well. Stir in nuts. Spread batter into prepared pan. Bake 35 to 40 minutes or just until brownies begin to pull away from sides of pan. Cool completely in pan on wire rack. Prepare Brownie Frosting; spread over brownies. Cut into bars. *About 3 dozen brownies*

Brownie Frosting

3 tablespoons butter or
    margarine, softened
3 tablespoons HERSHEY'S
    Cocoa
1⅓ cups powdered sugar

¾ teaspoon vanilla extract
1 tablespoon milk
1 tablespoon light corn syrup
    (optional)

In small bowl, beat butter and cocoa until blended; gradually add powdered sugar and vanilla, beating well. Add milk and corn syrup, if desired; beat until smooth and of spreading consistency. Add additional milk, ½ teaspoon at a time, if needed.

Fudge Cheesecake Bars

4 bars (1 ounce *each*)
    HERSHEY'S Unsweetened
    Baking Chocolate, broken
    into pieces
1 cup (2 sticks) butter or
    margarine
2½ cups sugar, divided
4 eggs
1 teaspoon vanilla extract

2 cups all-purpose flour
1 package (8 ounces) cream
    cheese, softened
1 package (13 ounces)
    HERSHEY'S HUGS
    Chocolates *or* HUGS
    WITH ALMONDS
    Chocolates, divided

Heat oven to 350°F. Grease 13×9×2-inch baking pan. In large microwave-safe bowl, place baking chocolate and butter. Microwave at HIGH (100%) 2 to 2½ minutes, or until butter and chocolate are completely melted, stirring after each minute. Beat in 2 cups sugar, 3 eggs and vanilla until blended. Stir in flour; spread batter into prepared pan. In small mixer bowl, beat cream cheese, remaining ½ cup sugar and remaining 1 egg until blended. Remove wrappers from 12 chocolate pieces. Coarsely chop; stir into cream cheese mixture. Drop batter by spoonfuls over top of chocolate mixture in pan. Swirl with knife for marbled effect. Bake 35 to 40 minutes or just until set. Cool completely in pan on wire rack. Cut into bars. Remove wrappers from remaining chocolate pieces; press onto tops of bars. Cover; refrigerate leftover bars. *About 3 dozen bars*

Top to bottom: Sachertorte Squares, Butterscotch Blondies (page 104)

Sachertorte Squares

1 cup (2 sticks) butter or
    margarine
1⅔ cups sugar
⅔ cup HERSHEY'S Cocoa
3 eggs
1½ teaspoons vanilla extract
1¼ cups all-purpose flour

¼ teaspoon baking powder
¼ teaspoon salt
½ cup apricot or seedless black
    raspberry preserves
Satiny Chocolate Glaze
    (recipe follows)
Sliced almonds

Heat oven to 325°F. Line 15½×10½×1-inch jelly-roll pan with wax paper or foil. In medium saucepan, melt butter. Add sugar and cocoa; stir until well blended. Remove from heat. Add eggs, one at a time, beating well after each addition. Stir in vanilla. Stir together flour, baking powder and salt; gradually add to chocolate mixture, beating until well blended. Spread batter into prepared pan. Bake 16 to 20 minutes or until top springs back when touched lightly in center. Cool 10 minutes; remove from pan to wire rack. Carefully remove wax paper. Cool completely. Cut in half lengthwise, then crosswise, forming 4 rectangles. Spread preserves over two rectangles. Top with remaining two rectangles. Cut into 1½-inch squares; place on wire rack with wax paper beneath to catch drips while glazing. Prepare Satiny Chocolate Glaze. Spoon glaze over squares, allowing glaze to run down sides. Garnish with almonds.   *2½ dozen squares*

Satiny Chocolate Glaze

2 tablespoons butter or
    margarine
3 tablespoons HERSHEY'S
    Cocoa

2 tablespoons water
1 cup powdered sugar
½ teaspoon vanilla extract

In small saucepan over low heat, melt butter. Add cocoa and water; stir constantly until mixture thickens. *Do not boil.* Remove from heat; gradually add powdered sugar and vanilla, beating with whisk until smooth and of desired consistency. Add additional water, ½ teaspoon at a time, if needed.

Butterscotch Blondies

¾ cup (1½ sticks) butter or
    margarine, softened
¾ cup packed light brown
    sugar
½ cup granulated sugar
2 eggs
2 cups all-purpose flour

1 teaspoon baking soda
½ teaspoon salt
1⅔ cups (10-ounce package)
    HERSHEY'S Butterscotch
    Chips
1 cup chopped nuts (optional)

Heat oven to 350°F. Grease 13×9×2-inch baking pan. In large mixer bowl, beat butter, brown sugar and granulated sugar until creamy. Add eggs; beat well. Stir together flour, baking soda and salt; gradually add to butter mixture, blending well. Stir in butterscotch chips and nuts, if desired. Spread into prepared pan. Bake 30 to 35 minutes or until top is golden brown and center is set. Cool completely in pan on wire rack. Cut into bars. *About 36 bars*

Double Chocolate Chip Brownies

½ cup (1 stick) butter or
    margarine, softened
¾ cup sugar
1 egg
½ cup dairy sour cream
1 teaspoon vanilla extract
1 cup all-purpose flour
¼ cup HERSHEY'S Cocoa

¼ teaspoon baking soda
¼ teaspoon salt
1 cup HERSHEY'S MINI
    CHIPS Semi-Sweet
    Chocolate
Easy Brownie Frosting
    (recipe follows)

Heat oven to 350°F. Grease 9-inch square baking pan. In bowl, beat butter, sugar and egg until light and fluffy. Add sour cream and vanilla; beat until well blended. Stir together flour, cocoa, baking soda and salt. Add to butter mixture; blend well. Stir in small chocolate chips. Spread batter evenly into prepared pan. Bake 30 to 35 minutes or until wooden pick inserted in center barely comes out clean. *Do not overbake.* Cool completely in pan on wire rack. Prepare Easy Brownie Frosting; spread over brownies. Cut into squares. *20 brownies*

Easy Brownie Frosting

3 tablespoons butter or
    margarine, softened
3 tablespoons HERSHEY'S
    Cocoa

½ teaspoon vanilla extract
1¼ cups powdered sugar
2 tablespoons milk

In small mixer bowl, beat butter and cocoa until blended. Add vanilla and powdered sugar; beat well. Gradually add milk, beating until smooth and of spreading consistency. Add additional milk, 1 teaspoon at a time, if needed.

Mini Chips Brownie Cookies

¼ cup (½ stick) butter or
    margarine, softened
⅔ cup sugar
1 egg
1½ teaspoons vanilla extract
2 cups (12-ounce package)
    HERSHEY'S MINI CHIPS
    Semi-Sweet Chocolate,
    divided

½ cup all-purpose flour
¼ teaspoon baking powder
¼ teaspoon salt
½ cup chopped nuts (optional)

Heat oven to 350°F. In small mixer bowl, beat butter and sugar until creamy. Add egg and vanilla; beat well. In small microwave-safe bowl, place 1 cup small chocolate chips. Microwave at HIGH (100%) 45 seconds; stir. If necessary, microwave at HIGH an additional 15 seconds at a time, stirring after each heating, just until chips are melted when stirred. Add to butter mixture; blend well. Stir together flour, baking powder and salt; gradually add to butter mixture, beating well. Stir in remaining 1 cup chips and nuts, if desired. Drop dough by teaspoonfuls onto ungreased cookie sheet. Bake 8 to 10 minutes or until almost set. Cool slightly; remove from cookie sheet to wire rack. Cool completely.

About 2½ dozen cookies

Mini Chips Brownie Bars: *Spread batter into greased 8- or 9-inch square baking pan. Bake at 350°F 25 to 30 minutes or until cookies begin to pull away from sides of pan. Cool completely in pan on wire rack. Cut into bars. Makes about 20 bars.*

Fudge Filled Walnut-Oatmeal Bars

1 cup (2 sticks) butter or
    margarine, softened
2 cups packed light brown
    sugar
2 eggs
1 teaspoon vanilla extract
½ teaspoon powdered instant
    coffee (optional)
3 cups quick-cooking rolled
    oats

2½ cups all-purpose flour
1 teaspoon baking soda
½ teaspoon salt
1½ cups chopped walnuts,
    divided
    Chocolate Filling (recipe
    follows)

Heat oven to 350°F. In large mixer bowl, beat butter and brown sugar until creamy. Add eggs, vanilla and instant coffee, if desired; beat well. Stir together oats, flour, baking soda, salt and 1 cup walnuts; gradually add to butter mixture, beating until blended. (Batter will be stiff; stir in last part by hand.) Remove 2 cups dough. Press remaining dough onto bottom of 15½×10½×1-inch jelly-roll pan. Prepare Chocolate Filling; spread over mixture in pan. Sprinkle reserved dough over chocolate. Sprinkle with remaining ½ cup walnuts. Bake 25 minutes or until top is golden. (Chocolate will be soft.) Cool completely in pan on wire rack. Cut into bars. *About 4 dozen bars*

Chocolate Filling

1 tablespoon butter or
    margarine
3½ bars (1 ounce *each*)
    HERSHEY'S Unsweetened
    Baking Chocolate, broken
    into pieces

1 can (14 ounces) sweetened
    condensed milk (*not*
    evaporated milk)
½ cup sugar
1½ teaspoons vanilla extract

In medium saucepan over low heat, melt butter. Add chocolate; cook until smooth and completely melted, stirring occasionally. Stir in sweetened condensed milk and sugar. Cook, stirring constantly, until mixture thickens and sugar is dissolved. Remove from heat. Stir in vanilla.

Fudge Filled Walnut-Oatmeal Bars

SENSATIONAL PIES & TARTS

Upside-Down Hot Fudge Sundae Pie

⅔ cup butter or margarine
⅓ cup HERSHEY'S Cocoa
2 eggs
¼ cup milk
1 teaspoon vanilla extract
1 cup packed light brown
   sugar
½ cup granulated sugar

1 tablespoon all-purpose flour
⅛ teaspoon salt
1 unbaked 9-inch pie crust
2 bananas, peeled and thinly
   sliced
Ice cream, any flavor
Whipped topping

Heat oven to 350°F. In medium saucepan over low heat, melt butter. Add cocoa; stir until smooth. Remove from heat. In small bowl, stir together eggs, milk and vanilla. Add egg mixture to cocoa mixture; stir with whisk until smooth and slightly thickened. Add brown sugar, granulated sugar, flour and salt; stir with whisk until smooth. Pour mixture into unbaked crust. Bake 30 to 35 minutes until edge is set. (Center will be soft.) Cool about 2 hours. Just before serving, top each serving with banana slices, ice cream and whipped topping. *8 servings*

Upside-Down Hot Fudge Sundae Pie

Chocolate & Vanilla Swirl Tart

Chocolate & Vanilla Swirl Tart

Tart Shell (recipe follows)
⅔ cup HERSHEY'S Semi-Sweet
    Chocolate Chips
½ cup milk, divided
2 tablespoons sugar
½ teaspoon unflavored gelatin

1 tablespoon cold water
⅔ cup HERSHEY'S Vanilla
    Milk Chips
1 teaspoon vanilla extract
1 cup (½ pint) cold whipping
    cream

Prepare Tart Shell. In small microwave-safe bowl, place chocolate chips, ¼ cup milk and sugar. Microwave at HIGH (100%) 1 minute; stir. If necessary, microwave at HIGH an additional 15 seconds at a time, stirring after each heating, just until chips are melted when stirred. Cool about 20 minutes. In small cup, sprinkle gelatin over water; let stand 2 minutes to soften. In second small microwave-safe bowl, place vanilla milk chips and remaining ¼ cup milk. Microwave at HIGH 1 minute; stir. Add gelatin mixture and vanilla; stir until gelatin is dissolved. Cool about 20 minutes. In small mixer bowl on high speed of electric mixer, beat whipping cream until stiff; fold 1 cup whipped cream into vanilla mixture. Fold remaining whipped cream into chocolate mixture. Alternately spoon chocolate and vanilla mixtures into prepared tart shell; swirl with knife for marbled effect. Refrigerate until firm. Cover; refrigerate leftover tart. *8 to 10 servings*

Tart Shell

½ cup (1 stick) butter (do *not*
    use margarine), softened
2 tablespoons sugar

2 egg yolks
1 cup all-purpose flour

Heat oven to 375°F. Grease bottom and sides of fluted 8- or 9-inch tart pan. In small mixer bowl, beat butter and sugar until blended. Add egg yolks; mix well. Stir in flour until mixture is crumbly. Press onto bottom and up sides of prepared pan. (If dough is sticky, sprinkle with 1 tablespoon flour.) Prick bottom with fork to prevent puffing. Bake 8 to 10 minutes or until lightly browned. Cool completely.

Top to bottom: Peanut Butter Crumble Topped Apple Pie (page 114), Our Gal Sundae Pie,
Chocolate Chunk Cookie Dough Cheesepie (page 114)

Our Gal Sundae Pie

Macaroon-Nut Crust (recipe
   follows)
⅔ cup packed light brown
   sugar
3 tablespoons all-purpose flour
2 tablespoons cornstarch
½ teaspoon salt
2¼ cups milk
½ cup HERSHEY'S Syrup
3 egg yolks, well beaten

2 tablespoons butter (do *not*
   use margarine)
1 teaspoon vanilla extract
   Sweetened whipped cream
   (optional)
   Maraschino cherries
   (optional)
1 HERSHEY'S Milk Chocolate
   Bar (1.55 ounces), broken
   into pieces (optional)

Prepare Macaroon-Nut Crust. In medium saucepan, stir together brown sugar, flour, cornstarch and salt. Gradually stir in milk, syrup and egg yolks until blended. Cook over medium heat until mixture comes to a boil, stirring constantly; boil 1 minute, stirring constantly. Remove from heat; stir in butter and vanilla. Pour mixture into prepared crust. Press plastic wrap directly onto surface. Cool on wire rack. Refrigerate at least 6 hours. Just before serving, garnish with sweetened whipped cream, maraschino cherries and chocolate bar pieces, if desired. Cover; refrigerate leftover pie.   *8 servings*

Macaroon-Nut Crust

1¼ cups coconut macaroon
   cookie crumbs (use
   purchased hard coconut
   macaroon cookies)

½ cup chopped walnuts
¼ cup (½ stick) butter (do *not*
   use margarine), melted

Heat oven to 350°F. In medium bowl, stir together cookie crumbs, walnuts and butter. Press firmly onto bottom and up sides of 9-inch pie plate. Bake 8 to 10 minutes or until lightly browned. Cool completely.

Chocolate Chunk Cookie Dough Cheesepie

Cookie Dough (recipe
 follows)
2 packages (3 ounces *each*)
 cream cheese, softened
⅓ cup sugar

⅓ cup dairy sour cream
1 egg
½ teaspoon vanilla extract
1 packaged chocolate crumb
 crust (6 ounces)

Prepare Cookie Dough. Heat oven to 350°F. In small mixer bowl on medium speed of electric mixer, beat cream cheese and sugar until smooth; blend in sour cream, egg and vanilla. Pour into crust. Drop cookie dough by teaspoonfuls evenly onto cream cheese mixture. Bake 35 to 40 minutes or just until almost set in center. Cool completely on wire rack. Cover; refrigerate leftover pie. *8 servings*

Cookie Dough

2 tablespoons butter or
 margarine, softened
¼ cup packed light brown
 sugar
¼ cup all-purpose flour

1 tablespoon water
¼ teaspoon vanilla extract
1 cup HERSHEY'S Semi-Sweet
 Chocolate Chunks

In small mixer bowl, beat butter and brown sugar until light and fluffy. Add flour, water and vanilla; beat until blended. Stir in chocolate chunks.

Peanut Butter Crumble Topped Apple Pie

1 cup (8 ounces) dairy sour
 cream
¾ cup sugar, divided
2 eggs
2 tablespoons plus ¾ cup
 all-purpose flour, divided
2 teaspoons vanilla extract
¼ teaspoon salt
4 cups peeled, thinly sliced
 apples (about 5 apples)

1 unbaked 9-inch pie crust
1 cup quick-cooking or regular
 rolled oats
1 teaspoon ground cinnamon
1 cup REESE'S Creamy Peanut
 Butter
1 tablespoon butter or
 margarine, softened

Heat oven to 350°F. In large bowl, with whisk, blend sour cream, ½ cup sugar, eggs, 2 tablespoons flour, vanilla and salt. Add apples; stir until well coated. Spoon into unbaked crust. Stir together oats, remaining ¾ cup flour, remaining ¼ cup sugar and cinnamon. In small microwave-safe bowl, place peanut butter and butter. Microwave at HIGH (100%) 30 seconds or until butter is melted. Stir mixture until smooth. Add to oat mixture; blend until crumbs are formed. Sprinkle crumb mixture over apples. Bake 55 to 60 minutes or until apples are tender and topping is golden brown. Cool completely on wire rack. Cover; refrigerate leftover pie.

6 to 8 servings

Hershey's Syrup Pie

2 egg yolks	1 baked 9-inch pie crust,
⅓ cup cornstarch	cooled, *or* packaged
¼ teaspoon salt	graham cracker crumb
1¾ cups milk	crust (6 ounces)
1 cup HERSHEY'S Syrup	Syrup Whipped Topping
1 teaspoon vanilla extract	(recipe follows)
	Fresh fruit

In medium microwave-safe bowl, beat egg yolks. Add cornstarch, salt, milk and syrup; blend well. Microwave at MEDIUM-HIGH (70%) 6 to 8 minutes or until mixture is smooth and very thick, stirring every 2 minutes with whisk. Stir in vanilla. Pour into prepared crust. Press plastic wrap directly onto surface. Refrigerate several hours or overnight. Just before serving, prepare Syrup Whipped Topping. Garnish pie with prepared topping and fruit. Cover; refrigerate leftover pie.

6 to 8 servings

Syrup Whipped Topping

½ cup cold whipping cream	1 tablespoon powdered sugar
¼ cup HERSHEY'S Syrup	¼ teaspoon vanilla extract

In small mixer bowl, combine whipping cream, syrup, powdered sugar and vanilla. Beat on high speed of electric mixer until stiff.

Fudgey Pecan Pie

⅓ cup butter or margarine
⅔ cup sugar
⅓ cup HERSHEY'S Cocoa
3 eggs
1 cup light corn syrup
¼ teaspoon salt

1 cup chopped pecans
1 unbaked 9-inch pie crust
Sweetened Whipped Cream
   (recipe follows)
Pecan halves (optional)

Heat oven to 375°F. In medium saucepan over low heat, melt butter. Add sugar and cocoa; stir until well blended. Remove from heat; cool. In medium bowl, beat eggs slightly. Stir in corn syrup and salt. Add cocoa mixture; blend well. Stir in chopped pecans. Pour into unbaked crust. Bake 45 to 50 minutes or until set. Cool completely on wire rack. Cover; let stand about 8 hours before serving. Prepare Sweetened Whipped Cream. Garnish pie with Sweetened Whipped Cream and pecan halves, if desired.

8 servings

Sweetened Whipped Cream

½ cup cold whipping cream
1 tablespoon powdered sugar

¼ teaspoon vanilla extract

In small mixer bowl, stir together whipping cream, powdered sugar and vanilla; beat on high speed of electric mixer until stiff.

Fudgey Mocha Pecan Pie: *In small bowl or cup, dissolve 1 teaspoon powdered instant coffee in 1 teaspoon hot water; add to pie filling when adding corn syrup and salt.*

Fudgey Pecan Pie

Clockwise from top: Chocolate Cherry Cheesepie, Fudgey Peanut Butter Chip Brownie Pie (page 120), Chocolate-Almond Pudding Tarts

Chocolate-Almond Pudding Tarts

¾ cup sugar
⅓ cup HERSHEY'S Cocoa
2 tablespoons cornstarch
2 tablespoons all-purpose flour
¼ teaspoon salt
1¾ cups milk
2 egg yolks, slightly beaten
2 tablespoons butter or
  margarine

¾ teaspoon vanilla extract
⅛ to ¼ teaspoon almond
  extract
6 single-serve graham cracker
  crumb crusts (4-ounce
  package)
Whipped topping
Sliced almonds

In medium microwave-safe bowl, stir together sugar, cocoa, cornstarch, flour and salt; gradually add milk and egg yolks, beating with whisk until smooth. Microwave at HIGH (100%) 5 minutes, stirring with whisk after each minute. Continue to microwave at HIGH 1 to 3 minutes or until mixture is smooth and very thick. Stir in butter, vanilla and almond extract. Spoon chocolate mixture equally into crusts. Press plastic wrap directly onto surface. Cool; refrigerate several hours. Just before serving, garnish with whipped topping and sliced almonds. Cover; refrigerate leftover tarts.

6 servings

Chocolate Cherry Cheesepie

2 bars (1 ounce *each*)
  HERSHEY'S Unsweetened
  Baking Chocolate, broken
  into pieces
4 packages (3 ounces *each*)
  cream cheese, softened
1¼ cups sugar
3 eggs

½ teaspoon vanilla extract
1 extra serving-size packaged
  graham cracker crust
  (9 ounces)
Sour Cream Topping
  (page 120)
1 can (21 ounces) cherry pie
  filling, chilled

continued on page 120

Chocolate Cherry Cheesepie (continued)

Heat oven to 375°F. In small microwave-safe bowl, place chocolate. Microwave at HIGH (100%) 1 to 1½ minutes or until chocolate is melted and smooth when stirred. Cool. In small mixer bowl on medium speed of electric mixer, beat cream cheese and sugar until smooth. Add eggs; beat well. Stir in vanilla and melted chocolate until completely blended. Pour into crust. Bake 20 minutes or until almost set in center. Remove from oven. Prepare Sour Cream Topping; spread over filling. Continue baking 10 minutes or just until set. Remove from oven to wire rack. Cool completely. Cover; refrigerate until firm. Just before serving, spread cherry pie filling over top of pie. Refrigerate leftover pie.

10 to 12 servings

Sour Cream Topping

1 cup dairy sour cream   ½ teaspoon vanilla extract
⅓ cup sugar

In small bowl, combine sour cream, sugar and vanilla; blend well.

Fudgey Peanut Butter Chip Brownie Pie

2 eggs
1 teaspoon vanilla extract
1 cup sugar
½ cup (1 stick) butter or margarine, melted
½ cup all-purpose flour
⅓ cup HERSHEY'S Cocoa
¼ teaspoon salt

⅔ cup REESE'S Peanut Butter Chips
1 packaged butter-flavored crumb crust (6 ounces)
Peanut Butter Sauce (recipe follows)
Vanilla ice cream

Heat oven to 350°F. In small mixer bowl, lightly beat eggs and vanilla; blend in sugar and butter. Stir together flour, cocoa and salt. Add to egg mixture; beat until blended. Stir in peanut butter chips. Place crust on baking sheet; pour chocolate mixture into crust. Bake 45 to 50 minutes or until set. Cool completely on wire rack. Prepare Peanut Butter Sauce; serve over pie and ice cream.

8 servings

Peanut Butter Sauce

1 cup REESE'S Peanut Butter
   Chips
⅓ cup milk

¼ cup whipping cream
¼ teaspoon vanilla extract

In small saucepan over low heat, combine peanut butter chips, milk and whipping cream. Cook, stirring constantly, until chips are melted and mixture is smooth. Remove from heat; stir in vanilla. Serve warm.

Chocolate Mint Mousse Pie

1 teaspoon unflavored gelatin
1 tablespoon cold water
2 tablespoons boiling water
½ cup sugar
⅓ cup HERSHEY'S Cocoa or
   HERSHEY'S European
   Style Cocoa

1 cup (½ pint) cold whipping
   cream
1 teaspoon vanilla extract
1 baked 8- or 9-inch pie crust,
   cooled
Mint Cream Topping (recipe
   follows)

In small cup, sprinkle gelatin over cold water; let stand 2 minutes to soften. Add boiling water; stir until gelatin is completely dissolved and mixture is clear. Cool slightly, about 5 minutes. Meanwhile, in small mixer bowl, stir together sugar and cocoa; add whipping cream and vanilla. Beat on medium speed of electric mixer until stiff, scraping bottom of bowl occasionally. Add gelatin mixture; beat just until blended. Pour into prepared crust. Prepare Mint Cream Topping; spread over filling. Refrigerate about 2 hours. Garnish as desired. Cover; refrigerate leftover pie.

6 to 8 servings

Mint Cream Topping

1 cup (½ pint) cold whipping
   cream
2 tablespoons powdered sugar

¼ to ½ teaspoon peppermint
   extract
Green food color

In small mixer bowl on medium speed of electric mixer, beat whipping cream, powdered sugar, peppermint extract and several drops green food color until stiff.

Secret Chocolate Strawberry Pie

3 cups sliced fresh
strawberries (about
2½ pints), divided
1 cup sugar
2 teaspoons cornstarch
1 package (3 ounces)
strawberry-flavored gelatin
1 tablespoon butter or
margarine
1 tablespoon lemon juice
¼ cup HERSHEY'S Semi-Sweet
Chocolate Chips

4 tablespoons whipping cream,
divided
1 baked 9-inch pie crust,
cooled
1 package (3 ounces) cream
cheese, softened
Sweetened whipped cream
(optional)
Whole strawberries
(optional)

Reserve 2 cups sliced strawberries. Mash remaining 1 cup sliced strawberries; add enough water to make 2 cups. In medium saucepan, stir together sugar and cornstarch; stir in mashed strawberries. Cook over medium heat until mixture comes to a boil, stirring constantly; cook 2 minutes, stirring constantly. Remove from heat. Add gelatin, butter and lemon juice; stir until gelatin is dissolved. Strain mixture; discard seeds. Refrigerate until partially set. Meanwhile, in small microwave-safe bowl, place chocolate chips and 3 tablespoons whipping cream. Microwave at HIGH (100%) 1 minute; stir. If necessary, microwave at HIGH an additional 15 seconds at a time, stirring after each heating, just until chips are melted when stirred. Spread chocolate mixture onto bottom of prepared crust; refrigerate 30 minutes or until firm. In small mixer bowl, beat cream cheese and remaining 1 tablespoon whipping cream until smooth; spread over chocolate layer. Refrigerate filled crust while gelatin mixture is cooling. When gelatin mixture is partially set, fold in reserved sliced strawberries; spoon mixture over cream cheese layer. Cover; refrigerate several hours or until firm. Just before serving, garnish with sweetened whipped cream and whole strawberries, if desired. Refrigerate leftover pie.

8 servings

Secret Chocolate Strawberry Pie

Strawberry Chiffon Pie

Chocolate Pastry (recipe
follows)
1 package (3 ounces)
strawberry-flavored gelatin
¾ cup boiling water
1½ cups chopped fresh
strawberries

2 cups frozen non-dairy
whipped topping, thawed
½ cup HERSHEY'S Semi-Sweet
Chocolate Chips
1 teaspoon shortening (do *not*
use butter, margarine or oil)
8 whole strawberries

Prepare Chocolate Pastry. In medium bowl, dissolve gelatin in water; cool slightly. Crush strawberries or purée to equal ¾ cup. Stir strawberry purée into gelatin mixture; refrigerate until partially set. (Mixture should be consistency of unbeaten egg whites.) Fold whipped topping into strawberry mixture. Spoon into prepared crust. Refrigerate 2 to 3 hours or until set. Line tray with wax paper. In small microwave-safe bowl, place chocolate chips and shortening. Microwave at HIGH (100%) 1 minute; stir. If necessary, microwave at HIGH an additional 15 seconds at a time, stirring after each heating, just until chips are melted when stirred. Dip whole strawberries into melted chocolate; place on prepared tray. Refrigerate, uncovered, about 30 minutes or until chocolate is firm. Just before serving, garnish pie with chocolate-covered strawberries. Cover; refrigerate leftover pie.

8 servings

Chocolate Pastry

1¼ cups all-purpose flour
¼ cup sugar
3 tablespoons HERSHEY'S
Cocoa

¼ teaspoon salt
⅓ cup vegetable oil
3 tablespoons cold water

In medium bowl, stir together flour, sugar, cocoa and salt. In measuring cup, place oil; add water. *Do not stir.* Pour liquid over flour mixture; stir lightly with fork until well blended. (If mixture is too dry, add 1 to 2 teaspoons additional cold water.) With hands, shape mixture into ball. Place between two pieces of wax paper; roll into 12-inch circle. Peel off top sheet of paper. Gently invert pastry over 9-inch pie plate; peel off paper. Fit pastry into pie plate. Fold under extra pastry around edge; flute edge. With fork, prick bottom and sides of crust thoroughly. Refrigerate about 30 minutes. Meanwhile, heat oven to 450°F. Bake 10 minutes. Cool completely.

Top to bottom: Frosty Chocolate Chip Pie (page 128), Chocolate Mint Mousse Pie (page 121), Strawberry Chiffon Pie

Chocolate Strawberry Fruit Tart

Chocolate Strawberry Fruit Tart

1⅓ cups all-purpose flour
½ cup powdered sugar
¼ cup HERSHEY'S Cocoa or
    HERSHEY'S European
    Style Cocoa
¾ cup (1½ sticks) butter or
    margarine, softened
Strawberry Vanilla Filling
    (recipe follows)

½ cup HERSHEY'S Semi-Sweet
    Chocolate Chips
1 tablespoon shortening (do
    not use butter, margarine
    or oil)
Glazed Fruit Topping
    (page 128)
Fresh fruit, sliced

Heat oven to 325°F. Grease and flour 12-inch pizza pan. In medium bowl, stir together flour, powdered sugar and cocoa. With pastry blender, cut in butter until mixture holds together; press into prepared pan. Bake 10 to 15 minutes or until crust is set. Cool completely. Prepare Strawberry Vanilla Filling; spread over crust to within 1 inch of edge; refrigerate until filling is firm. In small microwave-safe bowl, place chocolate chips and shortening. Microwave at HIGH (100%) 30 seconds; stir. If necessary, microwave at HIGH an additional 15 seconds at a time, stirring after each heating, just until chips are melted when stirred. Spoon chocolate into disposable pastry bag or corner of heavy duty plastic bag; cut off small piece at corner. Squeeze chocolate onto outer edge of filling in decorative design; refrigerate until chocolate is firm. Prepare Glazed Fruit Topping. Arrange fresh fruit over filling; carefully brush prepared topping over fruit. Refrigerate until ready to serve. Cover; refrigerate leftover tart. *12 servings*

Strawberry Vanilla Filling

1⅔ cups (10-ounce package)
    HERSHEY'S Vanilla Milk
    Chips
¼ cup evaporated milk

1 package (8 ounces) cream
    cheese, softened
1 teaspoon strawberry extract
2 drops red food color

In medium microwave-safe bowl, place vanilla milk chips and evaporated milk. Microwave at HIGH (100%) 1 minute; stir. If necessary, microwave at HIGH an additional 15 seconds at a time, stirring after each heating, just until chips are melted when stirred. Beat in cream cheese, strawberry extract and red food color.

continued on page 128

Chocolate Strawberry Fruit Tart (continued)

Glazed Fruit Topping

¼ teaspoon unflavored gelatin
1 teaspoon cold water
1½ teaspoons cornstarch *or*
  arrowroot

¼ cup apricot nectar *or* orange
  juice
2 tablespoons sugar
½ teaspoon lemon juice

In small cup, sprinkle gelatin over water; let stand 2 minutes to soften. In small saucepan, stir together cornstarch, apricot nectar, sugar and lemon juice. Cook over medium heat, stirring constantly, until mixture is thickened. Remove from heat; immediately stir in gelatin until smooth. Cool slightly.

Frosty Chocolate Chip Pie

1 cup HERSHEY'S Semi-Sweet
  Chocolate Chips
⅓ cup milk
1 package (3 ounces) cream
  cheese, softened
2½ cups frozen non-dairy
  whipped topping, thawed

1 baked 8-inch pie crust,
  cooled, *or* packaged crumb
  crust (6 ounces)
Additional whipped topping
Fresh fruit

In medium microwave-safe bowl, place chocolate chips and milk. Microwave at HIGH (100%) 1½ minutes; stir. If necessary, microwave at HIGH an additional 15 seconds at a time, stirring after each heating, just until chips are melted when stirred. With whisk or spoon, beat in cream cheese until mixture is well blended and smooth. Cool just to room temperature. Gradually fold 2½ cups whipped topping into chocolate mixture; spoon into prepared crust. Cover; freeze until firm. Garnish with additional whipped topping and fruit. Freeze leftover pie.

6 to 8 servings

Triple Chocolate Brownie Pie

2 eggs
1 cup sugar
½ cup (1 stick) butter or
    margarine, melted
½ cup all-purpose flour
⅓ cup HERSHEY'S Cocoa
¼ teaspoon salt

½ cup HERSHEY'S Semi-Sweet
    Chocolate Chips
½ cup chopped nuts
1 teaspoon vanilla extract
    Vanilla ice cream
    HERSHEY'S Chocolate
    Shoppe Topping

Heat oven to 350°F. Grease 9-inch pie plate. In small mixer bowl, beat eggs; blend in sugar and butter. Stir together flour, cocoa and salt. Add to egg mixture; beat until blended. Stir in chocolate chips, nuts and vanilla. Spread batter into prepared pie plate. Bake 30 to 35 minutes or until set. (Pie will not test done in center.) Cool completely on wire rack. Serve with ice cream and topping.

6 to 8 servings

Quick & Easy Chocolate Chip Cherry Pie

1 can (21 ounces) cherry pie
    filling
1 tablespoon cornstarch
1 extra serving-size packaged
    graham cracker crumb
    crust (9 ounces)
1 package (8 ounces) cream
    cheese, softened
¼ cup sugar

2 eggs
½ teaspoon vanilla extract
½ teaspoon almond extract
½ cup HERSHEY'S Semi-Sweet
    Chocolate Chips *or*
    HERSHEY'S MINI CHIPS
    Semi-Sweet Chocolate

Heat oven to 350°F. In medium bowl, stir together pie filling and cornstarch until blended; pour into crust. In small mixer bowl, beat cream cheese, sugar, eggs, vanilla and almond extract until blended; pour over pie filling. Sprinkle chocolate chips evenly over top. Bake 35 to 40 minutes or until almost set in center. Cool completely on wire rack. Cover; refrigerate until firm. Refrigerate leftover pie.

8 to 10 servings

DELICIOUS DECADENT DESSERTS

Strawberry Chocolate Chip Shortcake

1 cup sugar, divided
½ cup (1 stick) butter or
    margarine, softened
3 eggs
2 teaspoons vanilla extract,
    divided
1½ cups all-purpose flour
½ teaspoon baking powder
1 cup HERSHEY'S MINI
    CHIPS Semi-Sweet
    Chocolate *or* HERSHEY'S
    Semi-Sweet Chocolate
    Chips, divided

2 cups (16 ounces) dairy sour
    cream
2 cups frozen non-dairy
    whipped topping, thawed
    Fresh strawberries, rinsed
    and halved

Heat oven to 350°F. Grease 9-inch springform pan. In large bowl, beat ½ cup sugar and butter. Add 1 egg and 1 teaspoon vanilla; beat until creamy. Gradually add flour and baking powder, beating until smooth; stir in ½ cup small chocolate chips. Press mixture onto bottom of prepared pan. In medium bowl, stir together sour cream, remaining ½ cup sugar, 2 eggs and remaining 1 teaspoon vanilla; stir in remaining ½ cup small chocolate chips. Pour over mixture in pan. Bake 50 to 55 minutes or until center is almost set and edges are lightly browned. Cool completely on wire rack; remove side of pan. Spread whipped topping over top. Cover; refrigerate. Just before serving, arrange strawberry halves on top of cake. Garnish as desired. Refrigerate leftover dessert.　　　　　*12 servings*

Strawberry Chocolate Chip Shortcake

Cocoa Black Forest Crêpes

3 eggs
¾ cup water
½ cup light cream or half-and-half
¾ cup plus 2 tablespoons all-purpose flour
3 tablespoons HERSHEY'S Cocoa
2 tablespoons sugar

⅛ teaspoon salt
3 tablespoons butter or margarine, melted and cooled
Cherry pie filling
Chocolate Sauce (recipe follows)
Sweetened whipped cream (optional)

In blender or food processor, place eggs, water and light cream; blend 10 seconds. Add flour, cocoa, sugar, salt and butter; blend until smooth. Let stand at room temperature 30 minutes. Spray 6-inch crêpe pan lightly with vegetable cooking spray; heat over medium heat. For each crêpe, pour 2 to 3 tablespoons batter into pan; lift and tilt pan to spread batter. Return to heat; cook until surface begins to dry. Loosen crêpe around edges; turn and lightly cook other side. Stack crêpes, placing wax paper between crêpes. Keep covered. (Refrigerate for later use, if desired.) Just before serving, place 2 tablespoons pie filling on each crêpe; roll up. Place crêpes, seam side down, on dessert plate. Prepare Chocolate Sauce; spoon over crêpes. Garnish with whipped cream, if desired.   *About 18 crêpes*

Chocolate Sauce

¾ cup sugar
⅓ cup HERSHEY'S Cocoa
¾ cup evaporated milk
¼ cup (½ stick) butter or margarine

⅛ teaspoon salt
1 teaspoon kirsch (cherry brandy, optional)

In small saucepan, combine sugar and cocoa; blend in evaporated milk, butter and salt. Cook over medium heat, stirring constantly, until mixture comes to a boil. Remove from heat; stir in kirsch, if desired. Serve warm. Cover; refrigerate leftover sauce.

Top to bottom: Crunchy Nutty Ice Cream Sundae (page 135), Cocoa Black Forest Crêpes

Chocolate Cups with Lemon Cream

¼ cup plus 2 tablespoons
  all-purpose flour
½ cup sugar
2 tablespoons HERSHEY'S
  Cocoa
2 egg whites
¼ cup (½ stick) butter or
  margarine, melted

Chocolate Coating (recipe
  follows)
Lemon Cream (recipe
  follows)
Freshly shredded lemon peel
  (optional)

Heat oven to 400°F. Grease and flour cookie sheet. In small mixer bowl, stir together flour, sugar and cocoa. Add egg whites and butter; beat until smooth. Drop teaspoonfuls of mixture onto prepared baking sheet; with back of spoon, spread thinly into 5-inch circles. Bake 6 to 7 minutes. Immediately remove from cookie sheet; place, top side down, on inverted juice glasses. Mold to form wavy edges. (If chocolate cracks, gently press together with fingers.) Let stand about 30 minutes or until hard and completely cool. Prepare Chocolate Coating. With small brush, coat inside of cups with prepared coating. Refrigerate 20 minutes or until coating is set. Meanwhile, prepare Lemon Cream; spoon scant ½ cup Lemon Cream into each cup. Garnish with shredded lemon peel, if desired. Cover; refrigerate leftover desserts.

About 6 filled cups

Chocolate Coating

¾ cup HERSHEY'S Semi-Sweet
  Chocolate Chips

1 teaspoon shortening (do
  not use butter, margarine
  or oil)

In small microwave-safe bowl, place chocolate chips and shortening. Microwave at HIGH (100%) 45 seconds; stir. If necessary, microwave at HIGH an additional 15 seconds at a time, stirring after each heating, just until chips are melted when stirred.

Lemon Cream

1 package (4-serving size)
    instant lemon pudding and
    pie filling mix
1 cup milk

⅛ teaspoon lemon extract
1½ cups frozen non-dairy
    whipped topping, thawed

In small mixer bowl, combine pudding mix, milk and lemon extract. Beat on low speed 2 minutes. Fold in whipped topping; refrigerate 30 minutes or until set.

Crunchy Nutty Ice Cream Sundaes

Peanut Butter Sauce (recipe
    follows)

Coconut Crunch (recipe
    follows)
1 pint vanilla ice cream

Prepare Peanut Butter Sauce and Coconut Crunch. Scoop ice cream into sundae dishes. Spoon prepared sauce over ice cream; sprinkle prepared crunch over top. Serve immediately. *4 to 6 servings*

Peanut Butter Sauce

1 cup REESE'S Peanut Butter
    Chips
⅓ cup milk

¼ cup whipping cream
¼ teaspoon vanilla extract

In medium saucepan over low heat, heat peanut butter chips, milk and whipping cream until chips are melted, stirring constantly. Remove from heat; stir in vanilla. Cool to room temperature.

Coconut Crunch

½ cup MOUNDS Sweetened
    Coconut Flakes
½ cup chopped nuts

1 tablespoon butter or
    margarine

Heat oven to 325°F. In shallow baking pan, combine all ingredients. Toast in oven 6 to 8 minutes or until mixture is very lightly browned, stirring occasionally. (Watch carefully.) Cool to room temperature.

Chocolate Mousse

1 teaspoon unflavored gelatin	1 cup (½ pint) cold whipping cream
1 tablespoon cold water	
2 tablespoons boiling water	1 teaspoon vanilla extract
½ cup sugar	
¼ cup HERSHEY'S Cocoa or HERSHEY'S European Style Cocoa	

In small cup, sprinkle gelatin over cold water; let stand 2 minutes to soften gelatin. Add boiling water; stir until gelatin is completely dissolved and mixture is clear. Cool slightly. In small mixer bowl, stir together sugar and cocoa. Add whipping cream and vanilla. Beat on medium speed of electric mixer, scraping bottom of bowl occasionally, until mixture is stiff. Add gelatin mixture; beat until well blended. Spoon into serving dishes. Refrigerate about 30 minutes before serving. Garnish as desired. Cover; refrigerate leftover desserts.   *4 servings*

Note: *For double recipe, use 1 envelope gelatin; double remaining ingredients. Follow directions above, using cold large mixer bowl.*

Chocolate Mousse Filled Croissants: *Prepare Chocolate Mousse according to directions. Cut 6 bakery croissants crosswise in half. Spread about ⅓ cup mousse onto each bottom half; replace top half of croissant. Refrigerate about 30 minutes. To serve, top filled croissants with desired flavor of canned fruit pie filling, if desired. Makes 6 servings.*

Chocolate Mousse Parfaits: *Prepare Chocolate Mousse according to directions. Alternately spoon mousse and sliced fresh fruit into parfait glasses. Refrigerate about 1 hour. Makes 5 to 6 servings.*

Pound Cake Torte: *Prepare Chocolate Mousse according to directions. Slice loaf pound cake crosswise into three layers. Spread mousse between layers and over top. Refrigerate 1 to 2 hours. Garnish with sliced nuts or fruit. Makes 8 to 10 servings.*

Clockwise from top left: Chocolate Mousse Filled Croissants,
Chocolate Mousse Parfaits, Chocolate Mousse

*Top to bottom: Creamy Chocolate Dipped Strawberries (page 140),
Rich Chocolate Glazed Cream Puffs*

Rich Chocolate Glazed Cream Puffs

1 cup water	Chocolate Cream Filling
½ cup (1 stick) butter or	(recipe follows)
margarine	Rich Chocolate Glaze
¼ teaspoon salt	(page 140)
1 cup all-purpose flour	Fresh strawberries (optional)
4 eggs	

Heat oven to 400°F. Lightly grease cookie sheet. In medium saucepan, heat water, butter and salt to full rolling boil; reduce heat to low. Add flour all at once; beat with spoon until mixture forms ball. Remove from heat. Add eggs, one at a time, beating well after each addition until mixture is smooth. Drop by spoonfuls to form 12 balls on prepared cookie sheet. Bake 35 to 40 minutes or until golden brown. While puffs are warm, horizontally slice off small portion of each top; reserve tops. Remove any pieces of soft dough from inside of puffs; cool puffs on wire rack. Prepare Chocolate Cream Filling and Rich Chocolate Glaze. Fill puffs with filling; replace tops. Drizzle with prepared glaze. Garnish with fresh strawberries, if desired.

12 servings

Chocolate Cream Filling

½ cup sugar	1 cup HERSHEY'S Semi-Sweet
⅓ cup all-purpose flour	Chocolate Chips
½ teaspoon salt	1 tablespoon butter or
2½ cups milk	margarine
2 egg yolks, slightly beaten	2 teaspoons vanilla extract

In medium saucepan, stir together sugar, flour and salt; gradually stir in milk. Cook over medium heat, stirring constantly, until mixture comes to a boil; boil 2 minutes, stirring constantly. Gradually stir half the mixture into egg yolks; return to saucepan. Cook, stirring constantly, 1 minute. Remove from heat; stir in chocolate chips, butter and vanilla until mixture is smooth. Pour into bowl; press plastic wrap directly onto surface. Cool; refrigerate 1 to 2 hours or until cold.

continued on page 140

Rich Chocolate Glazed Cream Puffs (continued)

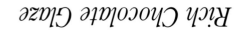

Rich Chocolate Glaze

½ cup HERSHEY'S Semi-Sweet Chocolate Chips	1 tablespoon shortening (do *not* use butter, margarine or oil)

In small microwave-safe bowl, place chocolate chips and shortening. Microwave at HIGH (100%) 1 minute; stir. If necessary, microwave at HIGH an additional 15 seconds at a time, stirring after each heating, just until chips are melted when stirred.

Note: For miniature cream puffs, prepare batter as directed. Drop batter by level teaspoonfuls onto lightly greased cookie sheet. Bake 15 minutes. Fill as directed.

Creamy Chocolate Dipped Strawberries

1 cup HERSHEY'S Semi-Sweet Chocolate Chips	Fresh strawberries, rinsed and patted dry (about
½ cup HERSHEY'S Vanilla Milk Chips	2 pints)
1 tablespoon shortening (do *not* use butter, margarine or oil)	

Line tray with wax paper. In medium microwave-safe bowl, place chocolate chips, vanilla milk chips and shortening. Microwave at HIGH (100%) 1 minute; stir. If necessary, microwave at HIGH an additional 15 seconds at a time, stirring after each heating, just until chips are melted when stirred. Holding top, dip bottom two-thirds of each strawberry into chocolate mixture; shake gently to remove excess. Place on prepared tray. Refrigerate about 1 hour or until coating is firm. Cover; refrigerate leftover dipped berries. For best results, use within 24 hours.

About 3 dozen dipped berries

Chocolate Lover's Mousse for Two

2 tablespoons sugar	1 tablespoon orange-flavored
½ teaspoon unflavored gelatin	liqueur, rum *or* 1 teaspoon
¼ cup milk	vanilla extract
½ cup HERSHEY'S MINI	½ cup cold whipping cream
CHIPS Semi-Sweet	Additional whipped cream
Chocolate	(optional)

In small saucepan, stir together sugar and gelatin; stir in milk. Let stand 2 minutes to soften gelatin. Cook over medium heat, stirring constantly, until mixture begins to boil. Remove from heat. Immediately add small chocolate chips; stir until melted. Stir in liqueur; cool to room temperature. In small mixer bowl on high speed of electric mixer, beat whipping cream until stiff. Gradually fold in chocolate mixture. Spoon into serving dishes. Refrigerate before serving. Garnish with additional whipped cream, if desired. *2 servings*

Note: *For high-standing mousse, prepare collars for two parfait glasses. Tear strip of foil of sufficient length to go around top of each glass. Fold foil lengthwise into fourths; butter lightly. Place buttered side in; tape to sides of glasses. Pour mousse into glasses. (Mousse should come over top of glass.) After mousse has set, carefully remove foil collar.*

Chocolate Fluted Kiss Cups

1½ cups HERSHEY'S MINI
    CHIPS Semi-Sweet
    Chocolate
    or 1 HERSHEY'S Milk
    Chocolate Bar (7 ounces),
    broken into pieces

Peanut Butter Filling (recipe
    follows)
24 HERSHEY'S KISSES Milk
    Chocolates

Line small muffin cups (1¾ inches in diameter) with small paper bake cups. In small microwave-safe bowl, place small chocolate chips. Microwave at HIGH (100%) 1 minute; stir. If necessary, microwave at HIGH an additional 15 seconds at a time, stirring after each heating, just until chips are melted when stirred. With small brush, coat inside of paper cups with melted chocolate. Refrigerate 20 minutes; coat any thin spots. Refrigerate until firm, preferably overnight. Gently peel paper from chocolate cups. Prepare Peanut Butter Filling; spoon into cups. Cover; refrigerate before serving. Remove wrappers from chocolate pieces. Before serving, top each cup with chocolate piece.   *About 24 servings*

Peanut Butter Filling

1 cup REESE'S Creamy Peanut
    Butter
1 cup powdered sugar

1 tablespoon butter or
    margarine, softened

In small mixer bowl, beat peanut butter, powdered sugar and butter until smooth.

Double Chocolate Delight

3 tablespoons butter or
   margarine, melted
2 tablespoons sugar
1 cup graham cracker crumbs
½ cup milk
1 HERSHEY'S Milk Chocolate
   Bar (7 ounces), broken
   into pieces

½ cup HERSHEY'S MINI
   CHIPS Semi-Sweet
   Chocolate
1 cup (½ pint) cold whipping
   cream
Sweetened whipped cream
Sliced sweetened
   strawberries

In small bowl, stir together butter and sugar. Add graham cracker crumbs; mix well. Press mixture firmly onto bottom of 8-inch square pan. Refrigerate 1 to 2 hours or until firm. Meanwhile, in small saucepan, heat milk just until it begins to boil; remove from heat. Immediately add chocolate bar pieces and small chocolate chips; stir until chocolate melts and mixture is smooth. Pour into medium bowl; cool to room temperature. In small mixer bowl on high speed of electric mixer, beat whipping cream until stiff; fold gently into chocolate mixture. Pour onto prepared crust; freeze several hours or until firm. Cut into squares. Just before serving, garnish with sweetened whipped cream and strawberries.

6 to 8 servings

Classic Chocolate Pudding

2 bars (1 ounce *each*)
   HERSHEY'S Unsweetened
   Baking Chocolate, broken
   into pieces
2½ cups milk, divided
1 cup sugar
¼ cup cornstarch
½ teaspoon salt

3 egg yolks, slightly beaten
1 tablespoon butter (do *not* use
   margarine)
1 teaspoon vanilla extract
Sweetened whipped cream
   (optional)
Pecan halves (optional)

continued on page 146

Top to bottom: Classic Chocolate Pudding, Double Chocolate Delight

Classic Chocolate Pudding (continued)

In medium saucepan, combine chocolate and 1½ cups milk; cook over low heat, stirring constantly with whisk, until chocolate is melted and mixture is smooth. In medium bowl, stir together sugar, cornstarch and salt; blend in remaining 1 cup milk and egg yolks. Gradually stir into chocolate mixture. Cook over medium heat, stirring constantly, until mixture comes to a boil; boil 1 minute, stirring constantly. Remove from heat; add butter and vanilla. Pour into bowl; press plastic wrap directly onto surface. Refrigerate 2 to 3 hours or until cold. Just before serving, garnish with whipped cream and pecans, if desired.

4 to 6 servings

Deep Dark Chocolate Soufflé

1 tablespoon sugar
½ cup HERSHEY'S European
    Style Cocoa
¼ cup all-purpose flour
¼ cup butter or margarine,
    softened

1 cup milk
½ cup plus 2 tablespoons sugar,
    divided
1 teaspoon vanilla extract
4 eggs, separated
Ice cream

Heat oven to 350°F. Butter 6-cup soufflé dish; lightly coat with 1 tablespoon sugar. In medium bowl, stir together cocoa and flour. Add butter; blend well. In medium saucepan, heat milk until very hot. *Do not boil.* Reduce heat to low. Add cocoa mixture; beat with whisk until smooth and thick. Remove from heat; stir in ½ cup sugar and vanilla. Cool slightly. Add egg yolks, one at a time, beating well after each addition. Cool to room temperature. In large mixer bowl, beat egg whites until foamy; gradually add remaining 2 tablespoons sugar, beating until stiff peaks form. Stir small amount of beaten whites into chocolate mixture; fold chocolate mixture into remaining whites. Carefully pour into prepared dish. Bake 40 to 45 minutes or until puffed. Serve immediately with ice cream.   *6 servings*

Brandied Cocoa-Nut Squares

½ cup (1 stick) butter or
    margarine
½ cup sugar
¼ cup HERSHEY'S Cocoa
1 teaspoon brandy extract
1 egg

1¾ cups vanilla wafer crumbs
    (about 50 wafers)
1 cup finely chopped walnuts
¾ cup flaked coconut
    Brandy-Cocoa Glaze (recipe
    follows)

In small saucepan, melt butter. Add sugar, cocoa, brandy extract and egg; beat with spoon until blended. Cook, stirring constantly, until slightly thickened. Remove from heat; stir in crumbs, walnuts and coconut. Press firmly onto bottom of ungreased 13×9×2-inch pan. Refrigerate, uncovered, until firm. Prepare Brandy-Cocoa Glaze; drizzle or spread over dessert. Refrigerate several hours or until firm. Cut into squares. *About 32 squares*

Brandy-Cocoa Glaze

1 cup powdered sugar
3 tablespoons HERSHEY'S
    Cocoa
3 tablespoons butter or
    margarine

½ teaspoon brandy extract
2 tablespoons boiling water

In medium bowl, combine all ingredients; stir until well blended.

Easy Chocoberry Cream Dessert

2 packages (3 ounces *each*)
   ladyfingers, split
1 package (10 ounces) frozen
   strawberries in syrup,
   thawed and drained
2 envelopes unflavored gelatin
2 cups milk, divided
1 cup sugar
⅓ cup HERSHEY'S Cocoa or
   HERSHEY'S European
   Style Cocoa

¼ cup (½ stick) butter or
   margarine
1 teaspoon vanilla extract
2 cups frozen non-dairy
   whipped topping, thawed
Additional whipped topping
   (optional)
Fresh strawberries (optional)
Mint leaves (optional)

Place ladyfingers, cut side in, on bottom and around sides of 9-inch springform pan. In food processor, purée strawberries. In medium saucepan, sprinkle gelatin over 1 cup milk; let stand 2 minutes to soften. Add sugar, cocoa and butter. Cook over medium heat, stirring constantly, until mixture is hot and gelatin is completely dissolved. Remove from heat; stir in remaining 1 cup milk, vanilla and puréed strawberries. Refrigerate until mixture begins to thicken. Fold 2 cups whipped topping into gelatin mixture. Pour mixture into prepared pan. Cover; refrigerate until mixture is firm. Just before serving, remove side of pan. Garnish with additional whipped topping, fresh strawberries and mint, if desired. Cover; refrigerate leftover dessert.   *10 to 12 servings*

Easy Chocoberry Cream Dessert

CELEBRATE THE HOLIDAYS

Chocolate-Nut Pinwheel Cookies

½ cup (1 stick) butter or margarine, softened
¾ cup sugar
1 egg
1 teaspoon vanilla extract
1¾ cups all-purpose flour
½ teaspoon baking powder
¼ teaspoon salt
⅓ cup ground almonds

1 tablespoon finely chopped, well-drained maraschino cherries
⅛ teaspoon almond extract (optional)
¼ cup HERSHEY'S Cocoa
4½ teaspoons butter or margarine, melted

In large mixer bowl, beat ½ cup softened butter and sugar until creamy. Add egg and vanilla; beat well. Stir together flour, baking powder and salt; gradually add to butter mixture, beating until mixture forms soft dough. Remove half the dough to medium bowl; blend in ground almonds, cherries and almond extract, if desired. Add cocoa and melted butter to remaining dough; blend well. Divide each dough in half. Refrigerate doughs, if necessary, until firm enough to handle. Between 2 pieces of wax paper, roll one portion almond dough into 8-inch square; repeat procedure with one portion chocolate dough. Remove top sheets of wax paper; invert almond dough onto chocolate dough. Peel off top sheet of wax paper; roll doughs up lightly. Repeat procedure with remaining doughs. Wrap both rolls in wax paper or plastic wrap; refrigerate 4 to 5 hours or until firm. Heat oven to 350°F. Cut rolls into ¼-inch-thick slices; place 2 inches apart on ungreased cookie sheet. Bake 9 to 12 minutes or just until set. Remove from cookie sheet to wire rack. Cool completely.   *About 5 dozen cookies*

Top to bottom: Jolly Peanut Butter Gingerbread Cookies (page 152), Cherry Vanilla Chip Brownies (page 156), Cheery Cherry Almond-Topped Fudge (page 152), Chocolate-Nut Pinwheel Cookies

Jolly Peanut Butter Gingerbread Cookies

1⅔ cups (10-ounce package)
  REESE'S Peanut Butter
  Chips
¾ cup (1½ sticks) butter or
  margarine, softened
1 cup packed light brown
  sugar

1 cup dark corn syrup
2 eggs
5 cups all-purpose flour
1 teaspoon baking soda
½ teaspoon ground cinnamon
¼ teaspoon ground ginger
¼ teaspoon salt

In small microwave-safe bowl, place peanut butter chips. Microwave at HIGH (100%) 1 minute; stir. If necessary, microwave at HIGH an additional 15 seconds at a time, stirring after each heating, just until chips are melted when stirred. In large mixer bowl, beat melted peanut butter chips and butter until well blended. Add brown sugar, corn syrup and eggs; beat until light and fluffy. Stir together flour, baking soda, cinnamon, ginger and salt; gradually add half the flour mixture to butter mixture, beating on low speed of electric mixer until smooth. With wooden spoon, stir in remaining flour mixture until well blended. Divide dough into thirds; wrap each third in plastic wrap. Refrigerate about 1 hour or until firm enough to roll. Heat oven to 325°F. On lightly floured surface, roll one dough portion at a time to ⅛-inch thickness; with floured cookie cutters, cut into holiday shapes. Place on ungreased cookie sheet. Bake 10 to 12 minutes or until set and lightly browned. Cool slightly; remove from cookie sheet to wire rack. Cool completely. Frost and decorate as desired.   *About 6 dozen cookies*

Cheery Cherry Almond-Topped Fudge

1 can (8 ounces) almond paste
1 can (14 ounces) sweetened
  condensed milk (*not*
  evaporated milk), divided
Few drops red food color
1¾ cups HERSHEY'S Semi-
  Sweet Chocolate Chips or
  1 package (10 ounces)
  HERSHEY'S Semi-Sweet
  Chocolate Chunks

Red candied cherry halves
Sliced almonds

Line 8-inch square pan with foil, extending foil over edges of pan. In small bowl, beat almond paste and ¼ cup sweetened condensed milk until blended. Add food color; beat until well blended. Refrigerate about 1 hour or until stiff. Spread mixture into prepared pan. In medium bowl, place chocolate chips and remaining sweetened condensed milk. Microwave at HIGH (100%) 1 minute; stir. If necessary, microwave at HIGH an additional 15 seconds at a time, stirring after each heating, just until chips are melted when stirred. Spread over almond paste layer. Cover; refrigerate until firm. Use foil to lift fudge out of pan; peel off foil. Cut fudge into squares; garnish with cherry halves and almonds. Store in tightly covered container in refrigerator.

About 4 dozen pieces

Raspberry Almond-Topped Fudge: *Substitute 1⅔ cups HERSHEY'S Raspberry Chips for chocolate chips or chunks.*

Holiday Chocolate Shortbread Cookies

1 cup (2 sticks) butter (do *not* use margarine), softened
1¼ cups powdered sugar
1 teaspoon vanilla extract
½ cup HERSHEY'S Cocoa or HERSHEY'S European Style Cocoa

1¾ cups all-purpose flour
1⅔ cups (10-ounce package) HERSHEY'S Vanilla Milk Chips

Heat oven to 300°F. In large mixer bowl, beat butter, powdered sugar and vanilla until creamy. Add cocoa; blend well. Gradually add flour, stirring until smooth. On lightly floured surface or between two pieces of wax paper, roll or pat dough to ¼-inch thickness; with cookie cutters, cut into holiday shapes. Reroll dough scraps, cutting cookies until all dough is used. Place on ungreased cookie sheet. Bake 15 to 20 minutes or just until firm. Immediately place vanilla milk chips, flat side down, in decorative design on warm cookies. Cool slightly; remove from cookie sheet to wire rack. Cool completely.

About 4½ dozen (2-inch-diameter) cookies

Note: *For more even baking, place similar shapes and sizes of cookies on same cookie sheet.*

Cheery Cranberry Chocolate Chip Bread

1 cup HERSHEY'S Semi-Sweet
   Chocolate Chips
1 cup fresh or frozen
   cranberries, coarsely
   chopped
½ cup chopped pecans
2 teaspoons freshly grated
   orange peel
2 cups all-purpose flour

1 cup sugar
1½ teaspoons baking powder
½ teaspoon baking soda
½ teaspoon salt
2 tablespoons shortening
¾ cup orange juice
1 egg, slightly beaten
   Cocoa Drizzle Glaze (recipe
   follows)

Heat oven to 350°F. Grease and flour three 5¾×3¼×2-inch foil miniature loaf pans. In small bowl, stir together chocolate chips, cranberries, pecans and orange peel. In large bowl, stir together flour, sugar, baking powder, baking soda and salt; with pastry blender, cut in shortening until mixture resembles coarse crumbs. Stir in orange juice, egg and reserved chocolate chip mixture just until dry ingredients are moistened. Spread evenly into prepared pans. Bake 40 to 45 minutes or until wooden pick inserted in center comes out clean. Cool 15 minutes; remove from pans to wire racks. Cool completely. Prepare Cocoa Drizzle Glaze; drizzle over top of loaves. *3 loaves (24 servings)*

Cocoa Drizzle Glaze

1 tablespoon butter or
   margarine
1 tablespoon HERSHEY'S
   Cocoa or HERSHEY'S
   European Style Cocoa

1 tablespoon water
½ cup powdered sugar
½ teaspoon vanilla extract

In small microwave-safe bowl, place butter. Microwave at HIGH (100%) 20 to 30 seconds until melted. Stir in cocoa and water. Microwave at HIGH 15 to 30 seconds or just until mixture is hot, slightly thickened and smooth when stirred. *Do not boil.* With whisk, stir in powdered sugar and vanilla until smooth and of desired consistency. Add additional water, a few drops at a time, if needed.

Chocolate Chip Fruit and Nut Bars

½ cup (1 stick) butter or
   margarine, softened
¾ cup packed light brown
   sugar
1 egg
½ teaspoon vanilla extract
1¼ cups all-purpose flour
½ teaspoon baking soda
½ teaspoon salt

Vanilla Butter Filling (recipe
   follows)
½ cup chopped candied red or
   green maraschino cherries
¼ cup chopped dried apricots
¼ cup raisins
¾ cup HERSHEY'S Semi-Sweet
   Chocolate Chips
½ cup coarsely chopped nuts

Heat oven to 350°F. Lightly grease 13×9×2-inch baking pan. In large mixer
bowl, beat butter, sugar, egg and vanilla until light and fluffy. Stir together flour,
baking soda and salt; gradually add to butter mixture, beating until blended.
Spread into prepared pan. Bake 12 to 15 minutes or until lightly browned. *Do not
turn oven off.* Cool crust about 5 minutes. Meanwhile, prepare Vanilla Butter
Filling; spread over crust. Sprinkle cherries, apricots, raisins, chocolate chips and
nuts over top. Continue baking 15 minutes or until center is set. Cool completely
in pan on wire rack. Cut into bars.   *About 36 bars*

Vanilla Butter Filling

2 tablespoons sugar
2 tablespoons milk
1 tablespoon butter or
   margarine, melted
1 egg

½ teaspoon vanilla extract
⅓ cup all-purpose flour
½ teaspoon baking soda
¼ teaspoon salt

In small mixer bowl, beat sugar, milk, butter, egg and vanilla until smooth. Add
flour, baking soda and salt; beat until well blended.

Cherry Vanilla Chip Brownies

½ cup chopped maraschino
    cherries, well drained
⅓ cup butter or margarine,
    softened
¾ cup sugar
2 eggs
2 tablespoons light corn syrup
1 tablespoon kirsch (cherry
    brandy) *or* 1 teaspoon
    vanilla extract and 1
    teaspoon almond extract
⅔ cup all-purpose flour

⅓ cup HERSHEY'S Cocoa or
    HERSHEY'S European
    Style Cocoa
¼ teaspoon baking powder
⅓ cup chopped slivered
    almonds
1 cup HERSHEY'S Vanilla
    Milk Chips
Vanilla Drizzle (recipe
    follows, optional)
Maraschino cherry halves,
    well drained (optional)

Heat oven to 350°F. Line 9-inch square baking pan with foil, extending foil over edges of pan. Grease and flour foil. Pat dry chopped cherries between layers of paper towels. In small mixer bowl, beat butter, sugar, eggs, corn syrup and kirsch until blended. Stir together flour, cocoa and baking powder; gradually add to butter mixture, beating until blended. Stir in chopped cherries, almonds and vanilla milk chips. Pour batter into prepared pan. Bake 25 to 30 minutes or until brownies begin to pull away from sides of pan. Cool completely in pan. Cover; refrigerate until firm. Use foil to lift brownies out of pan; peel off foil. Cut brownies into shapes with cookie cutters or cut into squares. Prepare Vanilla Drizzle, if desired; garnish brownies with drizzle and cherry halves, if desired. Refrigerate until drizzle is set. Cut into bars. Refrigerate leftover brownies.

About 16 brownies

Vanilla Drizzle

⅔ cup HERSHEY'S Vanilla
    Milk Chips

1 teaspoon shortening (do *not*
    use butter, margarine or oil)

In small microwave-safe bowl, place vanilla milk chips and shortening. Microwave at HIGH (100%) 30 seconds; stir. If necessary, microwave at HIGH an additional 15 seconds, stirring after each heating, just until chips are melted when stirred.

Chocolate Sweetheart Cakes for Two

¾ cup all-purpose flour
¼ cup granulated sugar
¼ cup packed light brown
    sugar
3 tablespoons HERSHEY'S
    Cocoa
½ teaspoon baking soda
⅛ teaspoon salt

½ cup water
3 tablespoons vegetable oil
½ teaspoon white vinegar
½ teaspoon vanilla extract
    Chocolate Frosting (recipe
    follows)
1 tube (4.25 ounces) pink
    decorating icing

Heat oven to 350°F. Grease and flour 8-inch square baking pan. In medium bowl, stir together flour, granulated sugar, brown sugar, cocoa, baking soda and salt. Add water, oil, vinegar and vanilla; beat with whisk until smooth. Pour batter into prepared pan. Bake 18 to 20 minutes or until wooden pick inserted in center comes out clean. Cool 10 minutes; remove from pan to wire rack. Cool completely. Transfer to cutting board. Using 3¼-inch heart-shaped cookie cutter, cut cake into four hearts. Prepare Chocolate Frosting; spread over tops of two hearts. Place remaining two hearts on top. Garnish with decorating icing. *2 small cakes*

Chocolate Frosting

1 tablespoon butter or
    margarine
⅔ cup powdered sugar
1 tablespoon HERSHEY'S
    Cocoa

2 teaspoons milk
⅛ teaspoon vanilla extract

In small microwave-safe bowl, place butter. Microwave at HIGH (100%) 20 seconds or until butter is melted. Stir together powdered sugar and cocoa; add to butter mixture alternately with milk, beating well after each addition until smooth. Stir in vanilla. Add additional milk, ½ teaspoon at a time, if needed.

Clockwise from top: Fudgey Valentine Cake, Chocolate & Vanilla Hearts (page 160),
Cocoa Cookie Hearts (page 161)

Fudgey Valentine Cake

⅔ cup butter or margarine,
   softened
1¾ cups sugar
2 eggs
1 teaspoon vanilla extract
1¾ cups all-purpose flour
¾ cup HERSHEY'S Cocoa or
   HERSHEY'S European
   Style Cocoa

1½ teaspoons baking soda
1 teaspoon salt
1½ cups dairy sour cream
   Pink Buttercream Frosting
   (recipe follows)
   Maraschino cherries
   (optional)

Heat oven to 350°F. Grease and flour two 9-inch heart-shaped pans.* In large mixer bowl, beat butter and sugar until creamy. Add eggs and vanilla; beat well. Stir together flour, cocoa, baking soda and salt; add to butter mixture alternately with sour cream, beating well after each addition. Beat 3 minutes on medium speed of electric mixer. Pour batter evenly into prepared pans. Bake 35 to 40 minutes or until wooden pick inserted in center comes out clean. Cool 10 minutes; remove from pans to wire racks. Cool completely. Prepare Pink Buttercream Frosting; spread between layers and over top and sides of cake. Garnish with cherries, if desired. *10 to 12 servings*

One 8-inch square baking pan and one 8-inch round baking pan (each must be 2 inches deep) may be substituted for heart-shaped pans. Prepare, bake and cool cake as directed above. Cut round layer in half, forming two half circles; place cut edge of each half circle against sides of square layer to form heart.

Pink Buttercream Frosting

½ cup (1 stick) butter or
   margarine, softened
4¼ cups powdered sugar

4 tablespoons milk
2 teaspoons vanilla extract
¼ teaspoon red food color

In small mixer bowl, beat butter until creamy. Gradually add powdered sugar alternately with combined milk and vanilla, beating well after each addition until smooth and of spreading consistency. Stir in food color. Add additional milk, 1 teaspoon at a time, if needed.

Chocolate & Vanilla Hearts

1 cup HERSHEY'S Semi-Sweet
    Chocolate Chips or
    HERSHEY'S Milk
    Chocolate Chips
2 tablespoons shortening (do
    not use butter, margarine
    or oil), divided

¾ cup HERSHEY'S Vanilla
    Milk Chips
¼ cup finely ground nuts

In small microwave-safe bowl, place chocolate chips and 1 tablespoon shortening. Microwave at HIGH (100%) 1 minute; stir. If necessary, microwave at HIGH an additional 30 seconds at a time, stirring after each heating, just until chips are melted when stirred. Spoon into heart-shaped ice cube tray or candy molds, filling each ½ full; tap molds to release air bubbles and smooth surface. Refrigerate 8 to 10 minutes to partially set chocolate. Meanwhile, in small microwave-safe bowl, place vanilla milk chips and 1 tablespoon shortening. Microwave at HIGH 1 minute; stir. If necessary, microwave at HIGH an additional 30 seconds, stirring after each heating, just until chips are melted when stirred; stir in nuts. Spoon over chocolate layer; tap to smooth surface. Refrigerate several hours or until firm. Invert tray or molds; tap lightly to release candies.

About 10 candies

Almond Hearts: *Add 2 or 3 drops almond extract to melted chocolate chips.*

Cherry Hearts: *Omit nuts; add ¼ cup finely chopped red candied cherries and 2 or 3 drops red food color to melted vanilla milk chips.*

Mint Hearts: *Add ¼ teaspoon mint extract and 2 or 3 drops red or green food color to melted vanilla milk chips.*

Cocoa Cookie Hearts

½ cup (1 stick) butter or
    margarine, softened
1 cup sugar
2 eggs
2 cups all-purpose flour
½ cup HERSHEY'S Cocoa

1 teaspoon baking powder
½ teaspoon baking soda
½ teaspoon salt
    Valentine Frosting (recipe
    follows)

In large mixer bowl, beat butter, sugar and eggs until light and fluffy. Stir together flour, cocoa, baking powder, baking soda and salt; gradually add to butter mixture, beating until blended. Cover; refrigerate dough until firm enough to handle. Heat oven to 350°F. On lightly floured surface, roll dough to ⅛-inch thickness; cut with heart-shaped cookie cutter. Place on ungreased cookie sheet. Bake 5 to 7 minutes or until no imprint remains when cookies are touched lightly in center. Cool 1 minute; remove from cookie sheet to wire rack. Cool completely. Prepare Valentine Frosting; spread onto cookies. Decorate as desired.

About 4 dozen cookies

Valentine Frosting

1½ cups powdered sugar
2 tablespoons butter,
    margarine or shortening

2 tablespoons milk
½ teaspoon vanilla extract

In small bowl, beat powdered sugar, butter, milk and vanilla until smooth and of spreading consistency. Add additional milk, 1 teaspoon at a time, if needed.

Pink Valentine Frosting: *Stir in 2 to 3 drops red food color, tinting as desired.*

Chocolate Valentine Frosting: *Stir 3 tablespoons HERSHEY'S Cocoa into powdered sugar. Proceed as directed above, increasing milk to 3 tablespoons.*

Minty Chocolate Shamrock Cookies

¾ cup (1½ sticks) butter or
    margarine, softened
1 cup sugar
¼ cup light corn syrup
1 egg
1 teaspoon vanilla extract
2 HERSHEY'S Cookies 'n' Mint
    Chocolate Bars (7 ounces
    each), broken into pieces

2 cups all-purpose flour
¼ cup HERSHEY'S Cocoa
2 teaspoons baking soda
¼ teaspoon salt
    Green decorating icing
    (optional)

In large mixer bowl, beat butter and sugar until creamy. Add corn syrup, egg and vanilla; beat until well blended. In medium microwave-safe bowl, place chocolate bar pieces. Microwave at HIGH (100%) 1 to 1½ minutes or until chocolate is melted when stirred. Stir into butter mixture. Stir together flour, cocoa, baking soda and salt; gradually add to chocolate mixture, blending well. Cover; refrigerate dough 1 hour or until firm enough to handle. Heat oven to 350°F. For each shamrock cookie, shape dough into three ½-inch balls. Place in triangular position on ungreased cookie sheet with approximately ¼ inch between balls. Using slightly smaller ball, form 1½-inch stem; add to base of cookie. Bake 8 to 10 minutes or until set around edges. Cool slightly; remove from cookie sheet to wire rack. Cool completely. Pipe decorating icing around edges of cookie, if desired.
About 8 dozen 2-inch cookies

Minty Chocolate Slice 'n' Bake Cookies: *Prepare dough as directed above. Shape into two rolls, each 2 inches in diameter. Wrap both rolls in wax paper or plastic wrap; refrigerate until firm enough to slice. Cut rolls into ¼-inch-thick slices; place 2 inches apart on ungreased cookie sheet. Bake and cool as directed above.*

Top to bottom: St. Patrick's Mint Layered Pound Cake (page 164),
Minty Chocolate Shamrock Cookies

St. Patrick's Mint Layered Pound Cake

1 frozen loaf pound cake
(16 ounces), partially
thawed
Few drops green food color
(optional)
1 container (8 ounces) frozen
non-dairy whipped topping
(3½ cups), thawed

1 HERSHEY'S Cookies 'n' Mint
Chocolate Bar (7 ounces),
chopped

With serrated knife, slice pound cake horizontally into four layers. Stir green food color into whipped topping, if desired; stir in chocolate bar pieces. Place bottom cake layer on serving plate; spread about 1 cup topping mixture over layer. Repeat layers, ending with topping mixture. Cover; refrigerate. Garnish as desired. Refrigerate leftover cake. *About 8 to 10 servings*

Passover Chocolate Banana Cake

6 eggs, separated
⅔ cup plus ¼ cup sugar,
divided
½ cup potato starch
¼ cup HERSHEY'S Cocoa

1 cup mashed ripe bananas
(2 to 3 medium)
½ cup sliced almonds

Heat oven to 350°F. Lightly grease 13×9×2-inch baking pan. In small mixer bowl, beat egg yolks with ⅔ cup sugar until thick and pale yellow in color. Stir together potato starch and cocoa; gradually add to egg mixture, beating until well blended. Stir in bananas. In large mixer bowl on high speed of electric mixer, beat egg whites until foamy. Gradually add remaining ¼ cup sugar, beating until stiff peaks form. Stir about ½ cup egg white mixture into cocoa mixture. Gently fold cocoa mixture into remaining egg white mixture. Spoon batter into prepared pan. Sprinkle almonds over top. Bake 25 to 30 minutes or until top springs back when touched lightly in center. Cool in pan on wire rack. (Cake will settle and pull away from edges of pan slightly during cooling.) Cut into squares. *About 12 to 15 servings*

Shamrock Parfaits

1 envelope unflavored gelatin
½ cup cold water
¾ cup sugar
½ cup HERSHEY'S Cocoa
1¼ cups evaporated skim milk

1 teaspoon vanilla extract
2 cups frozen whipped topping, thawed, divided
⅛ teaspoon mint extract
6 to 7 drops green food color

In medium saucepan, sprinkle gelatin over water; let stand 2 minutes to soften. Cook over low heat about 3 minutes or until gelatin is completely dissolved, stirring constantly. In small bowl, stir together sugar and cocoa; gradually add to gelatin mixture, stirring with whisk until well blended. Continue cooking over low heat until sugar is dissolved, stirring constantly. Remove from heat. Stir in evaporated milk and vanilla. Pour mixture into large bowl. Refrigerate about 20 minutes or until mixture mounds slightly when dropped from spoon, stirring occasionally. Fold ½ cup whipped topping into chocolate mixture. Divide about half of mixture evenly among eight parfait or wine glasses. Stir mint extract and food color into remaining 1½ cups topping; divide evenly among glasses. Spoon remaining chocolate mixture over topping in each glass. Garnish as desired. Serve immediately or refrigerate until serving time. Cover; refrigerate leftover parfaits.

About 8 servings

Independence Day Flag Cake

Independence Day Flag Cake

¾ cup (1½ sticks) butter or
    margarine, softened
1⅔ cups sugar
3 eggs
1 teaspoon vanilla extract
2 cups all-purpose flour
⅔ cup HERSHEY'S Cocoa
1¼ teaspoons baking soda

1 teaspoon salt
¼ teaspoon baking powder
1⅓ cups water
    Vanilla Buttercream Frosting
    (recipe follows)
½ pint blueberries
1 quart small strawberries, of
    uniform size

Heat oven to 350°F. Grease and flour 13×9×2-inch baking pan. In large mixer bowl, combine butter, sugar, eggs and vanilla; beat on high speed of electric mixer 3 minutes. Stir together flour, cocoa, baking soda, salt and baking powder; add alternately with water to butter mixture, beating on low speed after each addition just until blended. Pour into prepared pan. Bake 30 to 35 minutes or until wooden pick inserted in center comes out clean. Cool 10 minutes; remove from pan to wire rack. Cool completely. Place cake on oblong serving tray or foil-covered cardboard. Prepare Vanilla Buttercream Frosting; spread over top and sides of cake. Arrange blueberries in upper left corner of cake, creating a 5×4-inch rectangle. Arrange strawberries in rows for red stripes.   *12 to 15 servings*

Vanilla Buttercream Frosting

3 cups powdered sugar
⅓ cup butter or margarine,
    softened

2 tablespoons milk
1½ teaspoons vanilla extract

In large mixer bowl, combine powdered sugar and butter. Add milk and vanilla; beat until smooth and of spreading consistency. Add additional milk, 1 teaspoon at a time, if needed.

Pumpkin Face Surprise Cookies

⅔ cup butter or margarine,
    softened
¾ cup sugar
1 egg
1 teaspoon vanilla extract
2 cups all-purpose flour
⅓ cup HERSHEY'S Cocoa

1½ teaspoons baking powder
1 tablespoon milk
1 SYMPHONY Milk Chocolate
    Bar (7 ounces)
Orange decorating frosting

In large mixer bowl, beat butter, sugar, egg and vanilla until light and fluffy. Stir together flour, cocoa and baking powder; add alternately with milk to butter mixture, beating well after each addition. Divide dough into quarters. Shape each quarter into ball; flatten slightly. Wrap individually in plastic wrap. Refrigerate dough 1 to 2 hours or until firm enough to handle. Meanwhile, break milk chocolate bar into pieces on scored lines; cut each piece in half. Heat oven to 350°F. Working with one portion of dough at a time on floured surface, roll to about ⅛-inch thickness. Using 2-inch round cookie cutter, cut dough into even number of rounds. Place half the rounds on ungreased cookie sheet. Place one chocolate piece in center of each round. Place remaining rounds on top. Using tines of fork, seal edges. Bake 8 minutes or until set. Remove from cookie sheet to wire rack. Cool completely. With frosting, decorate tops of cookies to resemble pumpkin faces. *About 40 cookies*

Cauldron Dipped Apples

8 to 10 medium apples, stems
    removed
8 to 10 wooden ice cream
    sticks
2 cups (12-ounce package)
    HERSHEY'S Semi-Sweet
    Chocolate Chips
¼ cup shortening (do *not* use
    butter, margarine or oil)

⅔ cup REESE'S Creamy Peanut
    Butter
⅔ cup powdered sugar
    Peanut Butter Sugar (recipe
    follows)

Line tray with wax paper. Wash and dry apples; insert wooden stick into stem end of each apple. In medium saucepan over low heat, melt chocolate chips and shortening. Remove from heat. Add peanut butter; stir until melted and smooth. With whisk, blend in powdered sugar. Dip apples into chocolate mixture; twirl gently to remove excess coating. Prepare Peanut Butter Sugar; sprinkle over apples. Place on prepared tray. Refrigerate until coating is firm. Store in refrigerator.

8 to 10 dipped apples

Peanut Butter Sugar

3 tablespoons REESE'S Creamy or Crunchy Peanut Butter

⅓ cup powdered sugar
1 tablespoon granulated sugar

In small bowl, combine peanut butter, powdered sugar and granulated sugar.

Harvest Mini Chip Muffins

¼ cup (½ stick) butter or margarine
1 cup sugar
1 cup canned pumpkin
2 eggs
2¼ cups all-purpose flour
2 teaspoons baking powder
½ teaspoon baking soda

¾ teaspoon pumpkin pie spice
½ teaspoon salt
½ cup milk
1 cup HERSHEY'S MINI CHIPS Semi-Sweet Chocolate
½ cup chopped pecans

Heat oven to 350°F. Grease or line muffin cups (2½ inches in diameter) with paper bake cups. In large mixer bowl, beat butter and sugar until creamy. Add pumpkin and eggs; blend well. Stir together flour, baking powder, baking soda, pumpkin pie spice and salt; add alternately with milk to pumpkin mixture, beating after each addition just until blended. Stir in small chocolate chips and pecans. Fill muffin cups ⅔ full with batter. Bake 20 to 25 minutes or until wooden pick inserted in center comes out clean. Serve warm.

About 2 dozen muffins

Witch's Hat Chocolate Cupcakes

¾ cup (1½ sticks) butter or
    margarine, softened
1⅔ cups sugar
  3 eggs
  1 teaspoon vanilla extract
  2 cups all-purpose flour
⅔ cup HERSHEY'S Cocoa

1¼ teaspoons baking soda
  1 teaspoon salt
¼ teaspoon baking powder
1⅓ cups water
  Orange Cream Filling (recipe
    follows)

Heat oven to 350°F. Line muffin cups (2½ inches in diameter) with paper bake cups. In large mixer bowl, combine butter, sugar, eggs and vanilla; beat on medium speed of electric mixer 3 minutes. Stir together flour, cocoa, baking soda, salt and baking powder; add alternately with water to butter mixture, beating after each addition until just blended. Fill muffin cups ⅔ full with batter. Bake 20 to 25 minutes or until wooden pick inserted in center comes out clean. Remove from pans to wire racks. Cool completely. Prepare Orange Cream Filling. Cut 1½-inch cone-shaped piece from center of each cupcake; reserve. Fill each cavity with scant tablespoon prepared filling. Place reserved cake pieces on filling, pointed side up. Refrigerate before serving. Cover; refrigerate leftover filled cupcakes.

About 2½ dozen cupcakes

Orange Cream Filling

½ cup (1 stick) butter or
    margarine
1 cup marshmallow creme
1¼ cups powdered sugar
½ to 1 teaspoon freshly grated
    orange peel

½ teaspoon vanilla extract
2 to 3 teaspoons orange juice
  Red and yellow food colors
    (optional)

In small mixer bowl, beat butter until creamy; gradually beat in marshmallow creme. Gradually add powdered sugar, orange peel and vanilla, beating until blended. Add orange juice and food colors, if desired; beat until smooth and of desired consistency.

Clockwise from top: Jumbo Jack-o'-Lantern Brownie (page 172), Boo Bites (page 172),
Witch's Hat Chocolate Cupcakes

Boo Bites

¼ cup (½ stick) butter or
   margarine
30 large marshmallows *or*
   3 cups miniature
   marshmallows
¼ cup light corn syrup

½ cup REESE'S Creamy Peanut
   Butter
⅓ cup HERSHEY'S Semi-Sweet
   Chocolate Chips
4½ cups crisp rice cereal

Line cookie sheet with wax paper. In large saucepan over low heat, melt butter. Add marshmallows. Cook, stirring constantly, until marshmallows are melted. Remove from heat. Add corn syrup; stir until well blended. Add peanut butter and chocolate chips; stir until chips are melted and mixture is well blended. Add cereal; stir until evenly coated. Cool slightly. With wet hands, shape mixture into 1½-inch balls; place balls on prepared cookie sheet. Cool completely. Store in tightly covered container in cool, dry place. *About 4 dozen pieces*

Jumbo Jack-o'-Lantern Brownie

¾ cup (1½ sticks) butter or
   margarine, melted
1½ cups sugar
1½ teaspoons vanilla extract
 3 eggs
¾ cup all-purpose flour
½ cup HERSHEY'S Cocoa

½ teaspoon baking powder
¼ teaspoon salt
   Orange Buttercream Frosting
   (recipe follows)
   Decorating icing or gel and
   assorted candies

Heat oven to 350°F. Line 12-inch pizza pan with foil; grease foil. In medium bowl, stir together butter, sugar and vanilla. Add eggs; with spoon, beat well. Stir together flour, cocoa, baking powder and salt; gradually add to egg mixture, stirring until well blended. Spread batter into prepared pan. Bake 20 to 22 minutes or until top springs back when touched lightly in center. Cool completely in pan on wire rack. If desired, remove brownie from pan; peel off foil. Prepare Orange Buttercream Frosting; spread over top of brownie. Garnish as desired with decorating icing and candies to resemble jack-o'-lantern face.

12 to 15 servings

Orange Buttercream Frosting

3 tablespoons butter or
   margarine, softened
2 cups powdered sugar

2 tablespoons milk
½ teaspoon vanilla extract
   Red and yellow food colors

In small mixer bowl, beat butter until creamy. Gradually add powdered sugar, milk and vanilla, beating until smooth and of spreading consistency. Add additional milk, 1 teaspoon at a time, if needed. Stir in food colors for desired orange color.

Pumpkin Bread

2 cups (16-ounce can)
   pumpkin
1 cup vegetable oil
⅔ cup water
4 eggs
3½ cups all-purpose flour
3 cups sugar
2 teaspoons baking soda

1½ teaspoons salt
1 teaspoon ground cinnamon
1⅔ cups (10-ounce package)
   REESE'S Peanut Butter
   Chips
1 cup chopped nuts
1 cup raisins (optional)

Heat oven to 350°F. Grease and flour three 8½×4½×2½-inch loaf pans. In large bowl, stir together pumpkin, oil, water and eggs. Stir together flour, sugar, baking soda, salt and cinnamon; gradually add to pumpkin mixture, stirring until well blended. Stir in peanut butter chips, nuts and raisins, if desired. Pour evenly into prepared pans. Bake 55 to 65 minutes or until wooden pick inserted in center comes out clean. Cool 10 minutes; remove from pans to wire racks. Cool completely.   *3 loaves (36 servings)*

BOUNTIFUL BRUNCH BREADS

Easier Chocolate-Filled Braid

Chocolate Nut Filling
(page 176)
2½ to 2¾ cups all-purpose flour,
divided
2 tablespoons sugar
½ teaspoon salt
1 package rapid-rise yeast
½ cup milk

¼ cup water
½ cup (1 stick) butter or
margarine
1 egg, at room temperature
Vegetable oil
Powdered Sugar Glaze (page
189, optional)

Prepare Chocolate Nut Filling. Heat oven to 375°F. In large mixer bowl, stir together 1½ cups flour, sugar, salt and yeast. In small saucepan, combine milk, water and butter; over low heat, heat just until liquids are hot, 125°to 130°F. (Butter might not be melted.) Gradually add to dry ingredients; beat on medium speed of electric mixer 2 minutes. Add egg and 1 cup flour; beat 2 minutes. Stir in enough remaining flour to form stiff dough. Cover; let rest 10 minutes. Onto well-floured board, turn out dough; roll into 18×10-inch rectangle. Spread Chocolate Filling lengthwise down center third of dough. Cut 1-inch-wide strips diagonally on both sides of dough to within ¾ inch of filling. Alternately fold opposite strips of dough at angle across filling. Carefully transfer to greased baking sheet. Shape into ring; pinch ends together. Brush lightly with oil; let stand 10 minutes. Bake 20 to 25 minutes or until lightly browned. Remove from baking sheet to wire rack. Cool completely. Prepare Powdered Sugar Glaze, if desired; drizzle over braid.

10 to 12 servings

continued on page 176

Easier Chocolate-Filled Braid

Easier Chocolate-Filled Braid (continued)

Chocolate Nut Filling

¾ cup HERSHEY'S Semi-Sweet
    Chocolate Chips
2 tablespoons sugar
⅓ cup evaporated milk

½ cup chopped nuts
1 teaspoon vanilla extract
¼ teaspoon ground cinnamon

In small saucepan, stir together chocolate chips, sugar and evaporated milk. Over low heat, cook, stirring constantly, until chips are melted and mixture is smooth. Stir in nuts, vanilla and cinnamon. Cool completely.

Cocoa Applesauce Bread

1⅔ cups all-purpose flour
¾ cup sugar
⅓ cup HERSHEY'S Cocoa
1 teaspoon baking powder
1 teaspoon baking soda
1 teaspoon salt
¼ teaspoon ground cinnnamon

Dash ground nutmeg
½ cup shortening
2 eggs
1 cup applesauce
½ cup chopped pecans
Quick Vanilla Drizzle (recipe
    follows)

Heat oven to 350°F. Grease bottom only of 9×5×3-inch loaf pan. In large mixer bowl, stir together flour, sugar, cocoa, baking powder, baking soda, salt, cinnamon and nutmeg. Add shortening, eggs and applesauce; beat just until blended. Stir in pecans. Spoon mixture into prepared pan. Bake 50 to 55 minutes or until wooden pick inserted in center comes out clean. Cool 15 minutes; remove from pan to wire rack. Cool completely. Prepare Quick Vanilla Drizzle; drizzle over bread.
1 loaf (14 servings)

Quick Vanilla Drizzle

½ cup powdered sugar

1 tablespoon milk

In small bowl, stir together powdered sugar and milk until smooth and of desired consistency. Add additional milk, ½ teaspoon at a time, if needed.

Crumb-Topped Cocoa Banana Bread

Crumb Topping (recipe
   follows)
1½ cups all-purpose flour
1⅓ cups sugar
  6 tablespoons HERSHEY'S
    Cocoa
1 teaspoon baking soda
½ teaspoon salt

¼ teaspoon baking powder
¼ teaspoon ground cinnamon
  Dash ground ginger
  Dash ground mace
2 eggs
½ cup vegetable oil
1 cup mashed very ripe
  bananas (2 to 3 medium)

Prepare Crumb Topping. Heat oven to 350°F. Grease bottom only of 9×5×3-inch loaf pan. In large bowl, stir together flour, sugar, cocoa, baking soda, salt, baking powder, cinnamon, ginger and mace. Add eggs, oil and bananas; stir just until all ingredients are well blended. Spoon batter into prepared pan. Sprinkle with prepared topping. Bake 55 to 60 minutes or until wooden pick inserted in center comes out clean. Cool 10 minutes. Remove from pan to wire rack. Cool completely. Tightly wrap and refrigerate leftover bread. *1 loaf (14 servings)*

Crumb Topping

3 tablespoons all-purpose flour
2 tablespoons sugar
⅛ teaspoon baking powder

⅛ teaspoon ground cinnamon
1 tablespoon cold butter or
  margarine

In small bowl, combine flour, sugar, baking powder and cinnamon. With pastry blender, cut in butter until mixture resembles fine crumbs.

Top to bottom: Butterscotch Crescents (page 180), Chocolate Nut Apple Strudel

Chocolate Nut Apple Strudel

1 sheet (½ of 17½-ounce
    package) frozen puff
    pastry
1 cup finely shredded peeled
    apple
¾ cup ground pecans
½ cup vanilla wafer crumbs
    (about 15 wafers)
¼ cup HERSHEY'S Cocoa or
    HERSHEY'S European
    Style Cocoa

¼ cup (½ stick) butter or
    margarine, melted
⅓ cup sugar
2 eggs
½ teaspoon vanilla extract
2 teaspoons water
    Powdered Sugar Drizzle
    (recipe follows)
    Chocolate Chip Drizzle
    (page 180)

Thaw puff pastry according to package directions. Heat oven to 425°F. Sprinkle cookie sheet with cold water. In medium bowl, stir together apple, pecans, crumbs and cocoa. In small bowl, combine butter, sugar, 1 egg and vanilla. Add to apple mixture; blend well. With floured rolling pin, roll out pastry on lightly floured surface to 12×10-inch rectangle. Spoon apple mixture lengthwise down center of pastry. Lightly beat remaining 1 egg and water. Fold one side of pastry over apple mixture; brush long edge with egg mixture. Brush long edge of remaining side of pastry with egg mixture. Fold over filling; press edges together to seal. Place, seam side down, on prepared cookie sheet. Brush with remaining egg mixture. Bake 20 to 25 minutes or until golden brown. Cool about 20 minutes. Prepare Powdered Sugar Drizzle and Chocolate Chip Drizzle; drizzle over warm strudel.

10 to 12 servings

Powdered Sugar Drizzle

¾ cup powdered sugar

1½ teaspoons milk

In small bowl, stir together powdered sugar and milk until smooth and of desired consistency. Add additional milk, ½ teaspoon at a time, if needed.

continued on page 180

Chocolate Nut Apple Strudel (continued)

Chocolate Chip Drizzle

¼ **cup HERSHEY'S Semi-Sweet Chocolate Chips**

1½ **teaspoons shortening (do *not* use butter, margarine or oil)**

In small microwave-safe bowl, place chocolate chips and shortening. Microwave at HIGH (100%) 30 seconds; stir. If necessary, microwave at HIGH an additional 15 seconds at a time, stirring after each heating, just until chips are melted when stirred.

Butterscotch Crescents

½ **cup HERSHEY'S Butterscotch Chips**
¼ **cup MOUNDS Sweetened Coconut Flakes**
2 **tablespoons finely chopped nuts**

1 **can (8 ounces) refrigerated quick crescent dinner rolls**
Powdered sugar

Heat oven to 375°F. In small bowl, stir together butterscotch chips, coconut and nuts. Unroll crescent roll dough to form eight triangles. Lightly sprinkle 1 heaping tablespoon butterscotch mixture on top of each; gently press into dough. Starting at short side of each triangle, roll dough to opposite point. Place rolls, point side down, on ungreased cookie sheet; curve into crescent shapes. Bake 10 to 12 minutes or until golden brown. Sprinkle with powdered sugar. Serve warm.

8 crescents

Chocolate Quickie Stickies

8 tablespoons (1 stick) butter
   or margarine, divided
¾ cup packed light brown
   sugar
4 tablespoons HERSHEY'S
   Cocoa, divided
5 teaspoons water

1 teaspoon vanilla extract
½ cup coarsely chopped nuts
   (optional)
2 cans (8 ounces *each*)
   refrigerated quick crescent
   dinner rolls
2 tablespoons granulated sugar

Heat oven to 350°F. In small saucepan over low heat, melt 6 tablespoons butter; add brown sugar, 3 tablespoons cocoa and water. Cook over medium heat, stirring constantly, just until mixture comes to boil. Remove from heat; stir in vanilla. Spoon about 1 teaspoonful chocolate mixture into each of 48 small muffin cups (1¾ inches in diameter).* Sprinkle ½ teaspoon nuts, if desired, over chocolate mixture in each cup. Unroll dough. Separate dough into eight rectangles; firmly press perforations together to seal. Melt remaining 2 tablespoons butter; brush over rectangles. Stir together granulated sugar and remaining 1 tablespoon cocoa; sprinkle over rectangles. Starting at longer side, roll up each rectangle; pinch seams together to seal. Cut each roll into six equal pieces. Place in prepared muffin cups, cut sides down. Bake 11 to 13 minutes or until lightly browned. Remove from oven; cool 30 seconds. Invert onto cookie sheet. Let stand 1 minute; remove pans. Serve warm or cool. *4 dozen small rolls*

*Rolls can be baked in two 8-inch round baking pans. Heat oven to 350°F. Cook chocolate mixture as directed; spoon half into each pan. Prepare rolls as directed; place 24 pieces, cut side down, in each pan. Bake 20 to 22 minutes or until lightly browned. Cool and remove pans as directed above.

Orange Streusel Coffeecake

Cocoa Streusel (recipe
  follows)
¾ cup (1½ sticks) butter or
  margarine, softened
1 cup sugar
3 eggs
1 teaspoon vanilla extract
½ cup dairy sour cream

3 cups all-purpose flour
2 teaspoons baking powder
1 teaspoon baking soda
1 cup orange juice
2 teaspoons freshly grated
  orange peel
½ orange marmalade *or* apple
  jelly

Prepare Cocoa Streusel. Heat oven to 350°F. Generously grease 12-cup fluted tube pan or 10-inch tube pan. In large bowl, beat butter and sugar until creamy. Add eggs and vanilla; beat well. Add sour cream; beat until blended. Stir together flour, baking powder and baking soda; add alternately with orange juice to butter mixture, beating well after each addition. Stir in orange peel. Spread marmalade onto bottom of prepared pan; sprinkle half the streusel over marmalade. Carefully spread half the batter over streusel. Sprinkle remaining streusel over batter; spread remaining batter over streusel. Bake 1 hour to 1 hour 5 minutes or until wooden pick inserted in center comes out clean. With metal spatula, loosen cake from sides of pan; immediately invert onto serving plate. Serve warm or cool. Garnish as desired.

12 servings

Cocoa Streusel

⅔ cup packed light brown
  sugar
½ cup chopped walnuts

½ cup MOUNDS Sweetened
  Coconut Flakes (optional)
¼ cup HERSHEY'S Cocoa

In small bowl, stir together brown sugar, walnuts, coconut and cocoa, if desired.

Orange Streusel Coffeecake

Chocolate Dessert Waffles

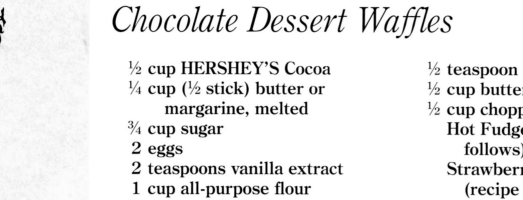

½ cup HERSHEY'S Cocoa
¼ cup (½ stick) butter or
    margarine, melted
¾ cup sugar
2 eggs
2 teaspoons vanilla extract
1 cup all-purpose flour
½ teaspoon baking soda

½ teaspoon salt
½ cup buttermilk or sour milk*
½ cup chopped nuts (optional)
    Hot Fudge Sauce (recipe
      follows)
    Strawberry Dessert Cream
      (recipe follows)

*To sour milk: Use 1½ teaspoons white vinegar plus milk to equal ½ cup.

In small mixer bowl, stir together cocoa and butter until smooth; stir in sugar. Add eggs and vanilla; beat well. Stir together flour, baking soda and salt; add alternately with buttermilk to cocoa mixture, beating after each addition just until blended. Stir in nuts, if desired. Bake in waffle iron according to manufacturer's directions. Carefully remove waffle from iron. Meanwhile, prepare Hot Fudge Sauce and Strawberry Dessert Cream; serve over warm waffles.

About ten 4-inch waffles

Note: *Leftover waffles may be frozen; thaw in toaster on low heat.*

Hot Fudge Sauce

¾ cup sugar
½ cup HERSHEY'S Cocoa
½ cup plus 2 tablespoons
    (5-ounce can) evaporated
    milk

⅓ cup light corn syrup
⅓ cup butter or margarine
1 teaspoon vanilla extract

In small saucepan, combine sugar and cocoa; stir in evaporated milk and corn syrup. Cook over medium heat until mixture comes to a boil, stirring constantly; boil 1 minute, stirring constantly. Remove from heat. Add butter and vanilla; stir until butter is melted. Serve warm.

Strawberry Dessert Cream

1 cup (½ pint) cold whipping
    cream
⅓ cup strawberry preserves

3 drops red food color
    (optional)

In small mixer bowl, beat whipping cream until stiff. Fold in strawberry preserves and food color, if desired.

Cocoa Streusel Cake

1 cup (2 sticks) butter or
    margarine, softened
2¼ cups granulated sugar,
    divided
2 eggs
1 cup (8 ounces) dairy sour
    cream
1 teaspoon freshly grated
    lemon peel
1 teaspoon fresh lemon juice

2 cups all-purpose flour
1 teaspoon baking powder
¼ teaspoon salt
1 cup chopped nuts
½ cup MOUNDS Sweetened
    Coconut Flakes
¼ cup HERSHEY'S Cocoa
1 teaspoon ground cinnamon
2 tablespoons butter or
    margarine, melted

Heat oven to 350°F. Grease and flour 12-cup fluted tube pan or 10-inch tube pan. In large mixer bowl, beat softened butter, 2 cups granulated sugar and eggs until light and fluffy. Add sour cream, lemon peel and lemon juice; beat until well blended. Stir together flour, baking powder and salt; gradually add to butter mixture, beating until well blended. Stir together nuts, coconut, cocoa, remaining ¼ cup granulated sugar and cinnamon; stir in melted butter. Pour half the cake batter into prepared pan; sprinkle with half the nut mixture. Carefully spread remaining batter over nut mixture; top with remaining nut mixture. Bake 1 hour or until wooden pick inserted in center comes out clean. Cool 10 minutes; remove from pan to wire rack. Cool completely. Sprinkle with powdered sugar, if desired.

12 to 16 servings

Clockwise from top left: Cocoa Cherry-Nut Snacking Bread, Nostalgia Date-Nut Loaf (page 188), Berry Loaf (page 188), Nostalgia Date-Nut Loaf (page 188)

Cocoa Cherry-Nut Snacking Bread

½ cup (1 stick) butter or
    margarine, softened
1 cup sugar
2 eggs
1 cup buttermilk or sour milk*
1¾ cups all-purpose flour
½ cup HERSHEY'S Cocoa
½ teaspoon baking powder
½ teaspoon baking soda
¼ teaspoon salt

½ cup finely chopped walnuts
½ cup finely chopped
    maraschino cherries,
    drained
Easy Vanilla Glaze (recipe
    follows, optional)
Maraschino cherries, halved
    (optional)
Walnut halves (optional)

To sour milk: Use 1 tablespoon white vinegar plus milk to equal 1 cup.

Heat oven to 350°F. Grease bottom only of 9×5×3-inch loaf pan. In large mixer bowl, beat butter, sugar and eggs until well blended. Blend in buttermilk. Stir together flour, cocoa, baking powder, baking soda and salt; gradually add to butter mixture, beating well. Stir in chopped walnuts and chopped cherries. Pour batter into prepared pan. Bake 55 to 60 minutes or until wooden pick inserted in center comes out clean. (Bread will crack slightly in center.) Cool 15 minutes. Remove from pan to wire rack. Cool completely. Prepare Easy Vanilla Glaze, if desired; drizzle over bread. Garnish with cherry halves and walnut halves, if desired.

About 12 servings

Easy Vanilla Glaze

1 tablespoon butter or
    margarine

½ cup powdered sugar
2 teaspoons hot water

In small microwave-safe bowl, place butter. Microwave at HIGH (100%) 30 seconds or until melted. Add powdered sugar. Gradually add water; stir until smooth and of desired consistency. Add additional water, ½ teaspoon at a time, if needed.

Nostalgia Date-Nut Loaves

1½ cups boiling water	2 teaspoons baking soda
1 cup dates, chopped	½ teaspoon salt
1¼ cups sugar	¼ teaspoon baking powder
1 egg	1 cup chopped walnuts
1 tablespoon vegetable oil	1 cup HERSHEY'S MINI
2 teaspoons vanilla extract	CHIPS Semi-Sweet
2 cups all-purpose flour	Chocolate

In medium bowl, pour water over dates; let stand 15 minutes. Heat oven to 350°F. Grease four 5¾×3¼×2¼-inch foil miniature loaf pans. In large mixer bowl on high speed of electric mixer, beat sugar, egg, oil and vanilla 3 minutes. Stir together flour, baking soda, salt and baking powder; add alternately with dates to egg mixture, beating well after each addition. Stir in walnuts and small chocolate chips. Pour evenly into prepared pans. Bake 40 to 50 minutes or until wooden pick inserted in center comes out clean. Cool 10 minutes; remove from pans to wire racks. Cool completely. Store, tightly wrapped, overnight before slicing.

4 loaves (32 servings)

Berry Loaf

2 cups all-purpose flour	1 egg, slightly beaten
1 cup sugar	1 cup chopped fresh
1½ teaspoons baking powder	cranberries
1 teaspoon salt	1 cup HERSHEY'S MINI
½ teaspoon baking soda	CHIPS Semi-Sweet
¾ cup orange juice	Chocolate
1 teaspoon freshly grated	¾ cup chopped nuts
orange peel	Powdered Sugar Glaze
2 tablespoons shortening	(recipe follows, optional)

Heat oven to 350°F. Grease 9×5×3-inch loaf pan. In large bowl, stir together flour, sugar, baking powder, salt and baking soda. Add orange juice, orange peel, shortening and egg; stir until well blended. Stir in cranberries, small chocolate chips and nuts. Pour batter into prepared pan. Bake 1 hour 5 minutes to 1 hour 10 minutes or until wooden pick inserted in center comes out clean. Cool 10 minutes; remove from pan to wire rack. Prepare Powdered Sugar Glaze, if desired; spread over top of loaf. Cool completely. Garnish as desired. *1 loaf (14 servings)*

Powdered Sugar Glaze

1 cup powdered sugar
1 tablespoon milk
1 teaspoon butter or
    margarine, softened

½ teaspoon vanilla extract

In small bowl, stir together powdered sugar, milk, butter and vanilla; beat until smooth and of desired consistency. Add additional milk, 1 teaspoon at a time, if needed.

Peanut Butter Chip Nutbread

½ cup shortening
¾ cup sugar
2 eggs
1¾ cups all-purpose flour
1 teaspoon baking soda
1 teaspoon salt
½ teaspoon ground cinnamon

¼ teaspoon ground nutmeg
1¼ cups applesauce
1⅔ cups (10-ounce package)
    REESE'S Peanut Butter
    Chips
½ cup chopped pecans
½ cup golden raisins

Heat oven to 350°F. Grease and flour 9×5×3-inch loaf pan. In large bowl, beat shortening, sugar and eggs until light and fluffy. Stir together flour, baking soda, salt, cinnamon and nutmeg; add alternately with applesauce to sugar mixture, mixing well after each addition. Stir in peanut butter chips, pecans and raisins. Bake 1 hour 15 minutes or until wooden pick inserted in center comes out clean. Cool 10 minutes; remove from pan to wire rack. Cool completely.

1 loaf (14 servings)

Cocoa Applesauce Raisin Muffins

1¼ cups all-purpose flour
½ cup whole-wheat flour
¾ cup packed light brown
    sugar
¼ cup HERSHEY'S Cocoa
1 tablespoon baking powder
½ teaspoon baking soda
½ teaspoon salt
¼ teaspoon ground cinnamon

⅛ teaspoon ground nutmeg
⅓ cup butter or margarine,
    melted
1 cup chunky applesauce
¼ cup milk
1 egg
¾ cup raisins
    Cinnamon Butter (recipe
    follows)

Heat oven to 400°F. Grease bottoms of or line muffin cups (2½ inches in diameter) with paper bake cups. In large bowl, stir together all-purpose flour, whole-wheat flour, brown sugar, cocoa, baking powder, baking soda, salt, cinnamon and nutmeg. In small bowl, stir together butter, applesauce, milk and egg until well blended. Add to dry ingredients; stir just until dry ingredients are moistened. Stir in raisins. Fill muffin cups about ¾ full with batter. Bake 20 to 22 minutes or until wooden pick inserted in center comes out clean. Remove from pans to wire racks. Cool slightly. Meanwhile, prepare Cinnamon Butter. Serve with warm muffins.

About 15 muffins

Cinnamon Butter

½ cup (1 stick) butter or
    margarine, softened
2 tablespoons powdered sugar

⅛ to ¼ teaspoon ground
    cinnamon

In small mixer bowl, beat butter, powdered sugar and cinnamon until well blended.

Clockwise from top left: Raspberry Chip Muffins (page 192), Cocoa Applesauce Raisin Muffins, Peanut Butter Chip & Banana Mini Muffins (page 192)

Raspberry Chip Muffins

1½ cups all-purpose flour
⅔ cup HERSHEY'S Raspberry
   Chips
½ cup sugar
2 teaspoons baking powder
½ teaspoon salt
½ cup chopped pecans
   (optional)
½ cup milk
¼ cup vegetable oil
1 egg
1 teaspoon vanilla extract

Heat oven to 400°F. Line muffin cups (2½ inches in diameter) with paper bake cups. In large bowl, stir together flour, raspberry chips, sugar, baking powder, salt and pecans, if desired. Stir together milk, vegetable oil, egg and vanilla. Add all at once to flour mixture; stir just until dry ingredients are moistened. Fill muffin cups ¾ full with batter. Bake 20 to 25 minutes or until lightly browned. Remove from pan to wire rack. Serve warm. *12 muffins*

Peanut Butter Chip & Banana Mini Muffins

2 cups all-purpose biscuit
   baking mix
¼ cup sugar
2 tablespoons butter or
   margarine, softened
1 egg
1 cup mashed very ripe
   bananas (2 to 3 medium)
1 cup REESE'S Peanut Butter
   Chips
Quick Glaze (recipe follows,
   optional)

Heat oven to 400°F. Grease small muffin cups (1¾ inches in diameter). In medium bowl, stir together baking mix, sugar, butter and egg; with fork, beat vigorously for 30 seconds. Stir in bananas and peanut butter chips. Fill muffin cups ⅔ full with batter. Bake 12 to 15 minutes or until golden brown. Meanwhile, prepare Quick Glaze, if desired. Immediately remove muffins from pan; dip tops of warm muffins into glaze. Serve warm. *About 4 dozen small muffins*

Quick Glaze

1½ cups powdered sugar   **2 tablespoons water**

In small bowl, stir together powdered sugar and water until smooth and of desired consistency. Add additional water, ½ teaspoon at a time, if needed.

Chocolate Chunks Peanut Butter Coffeecake

1⅔ cups (10-ounce package) REESE'S Peanut Butter Chips
2 tablespoons shortening (do *not* use butter, margarine or oil)
2¼ cups all-purpose flour
1½ cups packed light brown sugar
½ cup (1 stick) butter or margarine, softened

1 teaspoon baking powder
½ teaspoon baking soda
1 cup milk
3 eggs
1 teaspoon vanilla extract
1¾ cups (10-ounce package) HERSHEY'S Semi-Sweet Chocolate Chunks

Heat oven to 350°F. Grease bottom of 13×9×2-inch baking pan. In microwave-safe bowl, place peanut butter chips and shortening. Microwave at HIGH (100%) 1 minute; stir. If necessary, microwave at HIGH an additional 15 seconds at a time, stirring after each heating, just until chips are melted when stirred. In large mixer bowl, combine flour, brown sugar, butter and peanut butter chip mixture. Beat on low speed of electric mixer until mixture resembles small crumbs; reserve 1 cup crumbs. To remaining crumb mixture, add baking powder, baking soda, milk, eggs and vanilla; beat until well combined. Pour batter into prepared pan; sprinkle with reserved crumbs. Bake 35 to 40 minutes or until wooden pick inserted in center comes out clean. Remove from oven to wire rack; immediately sprinkle chocolate chunks over top. Cool completely.   *12 to 16 servings*

TANTALIZING TREATS

Chocolate Coconut Balls

3 bars (1 ounce *each*)
   HERSHEY'S Unsweetened
   Baking Chocolate, broken
   into pieces
¼ cup (½ stick) butter (do *not*
   use margarine)
½ cup sweetened condensed
   milk (*not* evaporated milk)

¾ cup granulated sugar
¼ cup water
1 tablespoon light corn syrup
1 teaspoon vanilla extract
2 cups MOUNDS Sweetened
   Coconut Flakes
1 cup chopped nuts
   Powdered sugar

In large heavy saucepan over low heat, melt chocolate and butter. Add sweetened condensed milk; stir to blend. Remove from heat. In small heavy saucepan, stir together granulated sugar, water and corn syrup. Cook over medium heat, stirring constantly, until sugar is dissolved. Cook, without stirring, until mixture reaches 250°F on candy thermometer or until syrup, when dropped into very cold water, forms a firm ball that does not flatten when removed from water. (Bulb of thermometer should not rest on bottom of saucepan.) Remove from heat; stir into chocolate mixture. Add vanilla, coconut and nuts; stir until well blended. Refrigerate about 30 minutes or until firm enough to handle. Shape into 1-inch balls; roll in powdered sugar. Store in tightly covered container in cool, dry place.

About 5 dozen candies

Note: *For best results, do* not *double this recipe.*

Clockwise from top left: Chocolate Coconut Balls, Peanut Butter Chip Brittle (page 196), Chocolate & Fruit Snack Mix (page 196)

Smooth Mocha Coffee

¾ cup hot brewed coffee
2 tablespoons HERSHEY'S
    Syrup

Whipped cream (optional)
Ground cinnamon (optional)

In mug or cup, stir together coffee and syrup. Garnish with whipped cream and cinnamon, if desired. Serve immediately.   *1 serving*

Chocolate & Fruit Snack Mix

½ cup (1 stick) butter or
    margarine
2 tablespoons sugar
1 tablespoon HERSHEY'S
    Cocoa or HERSHEY'S
    European Style Cocoa
½ teaspoon ground cinnamon
3 cups bite-size crisp rice
    squares cereal

3 cups bite-size crisp wheat
    squares cereal
2 cups toasted oat cereal rings
1 cup cashews
1½ cups (6-ounce package) dried
    fruit bits
1 cup HERSHEY'S Semi-Sweet
    Chocolate Chips

In 4-quart microwave-safe bowl, place butter. Microwave at HIGH (100%) 1 minute or until melted; stir in sugar, cocoa and cinnamon. Add cereals and cashews; stir until evenly coated. Microwave at HIGH 3 minutes, stirring after each minute; stir in dried fruit. Microwave at HIGH 3 minutes, stirring after each minute. Cool completely; stir in chocolate chips. Store in tightly covered container in cool, dry place.   *About 11 cups mix*

Peanut Butter Chip Brittle

1⅔ cups (10-ounce package)
    REESE'S Peanut Butter
    Chips, divided
1½ cups (3 sticks) butter or
    margarine

1¾ cups sugar
3 tablespoons light corn syrup
3 tablespoons water

Butter 15½×10½×1-inch jelly-roll pan.* Sprinkle 1 cup peanut butter chips evenly onto bottom of prepared pan; set aside. In heavy 2½-quart saucepan, melt butter. Add sugar, corn syrup and water. Stir constantly over medium heat until mixture reaches 300°F on candy thermometer. (Bulb of thermometer should not rest on bottom of saucepan.) Remove from heat. Immediately spread mixture into prepared pan; sprinkle with remaining ⅔ cup peanut butter chips. Cool completely. Remove from pan. Break into pieces. Store in tightly covered container in cool, dry place.   *About 2 pounds brittle*

Note: *For best results, do not double this recipe.*

For thicker brittle, use a 13×9×2-inch pan.

Peanutty Rocky Road

2 cups (12-ounce package) HERSHEY'S MINI CHIPS Semi-Sweet Chocolate
1 cup HERSHEY'S Milk Chocolate Chips
1 can (14 ounces) sweetened condensed milk (**not** evaporated milk)

1½ teaspoons vanilla extract
Dash salt
1⅔ cups (10-ounce package) REESE'S Peanut Butter Chips
1½ cups miniature marshmallows

Line 8-inch square pan with foil, extending foil over edges of pan. In large microwave-safe bowl, place small chocolate chips and milk chocolate chips. Microwave at HIGH (100%) 1½ minutes; stir. If necessary, microwave at HIGH an additional 30 seconds at a time, stirring after each heating, just until chips are melted when stirred. Stir in sweetened condensed milk, vanilla and salt; blend well. Fold in peanut butter chips and marshmallows. Immediately spread mixture into prepared pan. Refrigerate about 2 hours or until firm. Use foil to lift candy out of pan; peel off foil. Cut candy into squares.   *About 5 dozen pieces*

Top to bottom: Almond Cappuccino, Double Chocolate Truffles

Double Chocolate Truffles

½ cup whipping cream
1 tablespoon butter or
    margarine
4 bars (1 ounce *each*)
    HERSHEY'S Semi-Sweet
    Baking Chocolate, broken
    into pieces
1 HERSHEY'S Milk Chocolate
    Bar (7 ounces), broken
    into pieces

1 tablespoon amaretto
    (almond-flavored liqueur)
    or ¼ to ½ teaspoon almond
    extract
Ground almonds

In small saucepan, combine whipping cream and butter. Cook over medium heat, stirring constantly, just until mixture is very hot. *Do not boil.* Remove from heat; add chocolate, chocolate bar pieces and liqueur. Stir with whisk until smooth. Press plastic wrap directly onto surface; cool several hours or until mixture is firm enough to handle. Shape into 1-inch balls; roll in almonds to coat. Refrigerate until firm, about 2 hours. Store in tightly covered container in refrigerator.

About 2 dozen candies

Almond Cappuccino

1 tablespoon HERSHEY'S
    European Style Cocoa
1½ teaspoons sugar
1½ teaspoons powdered instant
    coffee

¾ cup milk
½ cup vanilla ice cream
¼ teaspoon almond extract

In small saucepan, combine cocoa, sugar and instant coffee; stir in milk. Add ice cream; heat to serving temperature. *Do not boil.* Stir in almond extract. Serve immediately. If desired, mixture may be placed in blender. Cover; blend until frothy.

1 serving

Orange Cappuccino: *Omit almond extract; add ¼ teaspoon orange extract and ¼ teaspoon vanilla extract.*

Champagne Cocoa Truffles

¾ cup (1½ sticks) butter (do *not* use margarine)
¾ cup HERSHEY'S Cocoa
1 can (14 ounces) sweetened condensed milk (*not* evaporated milk)

1 teaspoon vanilla extract
2 to 3 tablespoons champagne
Additional HERSHEY'S Cocoa *or* powdered sugar

Line tray with wax paper. In heavy 2-quart saucepan over low heat, melt butter. Add ¾ cup cocoa; stir until smooth. Add sweetened condensed milk; stir constantly until mixture is thick, smooth and glossy, about 4 minutes. Remove from heat; stir in vanilla. Pour mixture into medium bowl; cool to room temperature. Stir in champagne. Cover; refrigerate 4 to 5 hours or until firm. Working with small amount of mixture at a time, shape into 1¼-inch balls; roll in cocoa. Place balls on prepared tray; refrigerate until firm. Store in tightly covered container in refrigerator.   *About 2½ dozen candies*

Note: *For best results, do* not *double this recipe.*

Spanish Chocolate

2 cups (1 pint) light cream or half-and-half
4 HERSHEY'S Milk Chocolate Bars (1.55 ounces *each*), broken into pieces
¼ cup brewed coffee *or* ½ teaspoon powdered instant coffee dissolved in ¼ cup boiling water

Whipped cream (optional)
Crushed ice (optional)

In medium saucepan, combine light cream and chocolate. Cook over low heat, stirring constantly, until chocolate is melted and mixture is smooth. Stir in coffee. Beat with rotary beater or whisk until foamy. Serve hot with whipped cream, or cool and serve over crushed ice, if desired.   *5 servings*

Strawberry & Chocolate Shake

¼ cup sugar
3 tablespoons HERSHEY'S
    Cocoa
¼ cup water
½ cup cold milk

1½ cups sliced fresh
    strawberries
1 teaspoon vanilla extract
2 cups (1 pint) vanilla ice
    cream

In small microwave-safe bowl, stir together sugar and cocoa; stir in water. Microwave at HIGH (100%) 30 to 45 seconds until hot; stir until sugar is dissolved. Cool to room temperature. In blender, place cocoa mixture, milk, strawberries and vanilla. Cover; blend well. Add ice cream. Cover; blend until smooth. Serve immediately.

5 servings

Chocolate Nut Clusters

1 cup HERSHEY'S Milk
    Chocolate Chips
1 teaspoon shortening (do
    not use butter, margarine
    or oil)

1 cup broken pecans or
    walnuts

In medium microwave-safe bowl, place chocolate chips and shortening. Microwave at HIGH (100%) 1 minute; stir. If necessary, microwave at HIGH an additional 15 seconds at a time, stirring after each heating, just until chips are melted and mixture is smooth when stirred. Stir in nuts. Spoon heaping teaspoonfuls into 1-inch paper candy cups or paper-lined small muffin cups, filling each cup about ½ full. Refrigerate until firm. Peel off paper cups. Store in tightly covered container in refrigerator.

14 to 16 candies

Chocolate Mint Squares

6 tablespoons butter (do *not*
　use margarine)
½ cup HERSHEY'S Cocoa
2 cups powdered sugar

3 tablespoons plus 1 teaspoon
　milk, divided
1 teaspoon vanilla extract
　Mint Filling (recipe follows)

Line 8-inch square pan with foil, extending foil over edges of pan. In small saucepan over low heat, melt butter; add cocoa. Cook, stirring constantly, just until mixture is smooth. Remove from heat; add powdered sugar, 3 tablespoons milk and vanilla. Cook over low heat, stirring constantly, until mixture is melted and glossy. Spread half the mixture into prepared pan. Refrigerate. Meanwhile, prepare Mint Filling; spread over chocolate layer. Refrigerate 10 minutes. To remaining chocolate mixture in saucepan, add remaining 1 teaspoon milk. Cook over low heat, stirring constantly, until smooth. Spread quickly over filling. Refrigerate until firm. Use foil to lift candy out of pan; peel off foil. Cut candy into squares. Store in tightly covered container in refrigerator.

About 4 dozen candies

Mint Filling

1 package (3 ounces) cream
　cheese, softened
2 cups powdered sugar

½ teaspoon vanilla extract
¼ teaspoon peppermint extract
3 to 5 drops green food color

In small mixer bowl, beat all ingredients until smooth. Add 2 to 3 teaspoons milk, if needed, for spreading consistency.

Left to right: Chocolate Chip Peanut Butter Fudge (page 204), Hershey's Vanilla Milk Chips Almond Fudge (page 204), Chocolate Mint Squares

Chocolate Chip Peanut Butter Fudge

4 cups sugar
1 jar (7 ounces) marshmallow
   creme
1½ cups (12-ounce can)
   evaporated milk
1 cup REESE'S Creamy or
   Crunchy Peanut Butter

1 tablespoon butter or
   margarine
1 cup HERSHEY'S Semi-Sweet
   Chocolate Chips or
   HERSHEY'S Milk
   Chocolate Chips

Line 13×9×2-inch pan with foil, extending foil over edges of pan. Butter foil lightly; set aside. In heavy 4-quart saucepan, stir together sugar, marshmallow creme, evaporated milk, peanut butter and butter. Cook over medium heat, stirring constantly, until mixture comes to full, rolling boil; continue boiling 5 minutes, stirring constantly. Remove from heat. Immediately add chocolate chips; stir until smooth. Pour into prepared pan; cool until firm. Use foil to lift fudge out of pan; peel off foil. Cut fudge into pieces. Store in tightly covered container in cool, dry place. *About 8 dozen pieces or 3½ pounds candy*

Note: *For best results, do* not *double this recipe.*

Hershey's Vanilla Milk Chips Almond Fudge

1⅔ cups (10-ounce package)
   HERSHEY'S Vanilla Milk
   Chips
⅔ cup sweetened condensed
   milk (*not* evaporated milk)

1½ cups coarsely chopped
   slivered almonds, toasted*
½ teaspoon vanilla extract

*To toast almonds: Spread almonds in even layer on cookie sheet. Bake at 350°F 8 to 10 minutes or until lightly browned, stirring occasionally; cool.

Line 8-inch square pan with foil, extending foil over edges of pan. In medium saucepan over very low heat, melt vanilla milk chips with sweetened condensed milk, stirring constantly until mixture is smooth. Remove from heat. Stir in almonds and vanilla. Spread into prepared pan. Cover; refrigerate 2 hours or until firm. Use foil to lift fudge out of pan; peel off foil. Cut fudge into squares.

About 3 dozen pieces or 1½ pounds fudge

Note: *For best results, do* not *double this recipe.*

Double-Decker Cereal Treats

1⅔ cups (10-ounce package) REESE'S Peanut Butter Chips

2 tablespoons vegetable oil

2 teaspoons vanilla extract, divided

2 cups (12-ounce package) HERSHEY'S Semi-Sweet Chocolate Chips

2 cups light corn syrup

1⅓ cups packed light brown sugar

12 cups crisp rice cereal, divided

Line 15½×10½×1-inch jelly-roll pan with foil, extending foil over edges of pan. In large bowl, place peanut butter chips, oil and 1 teaspoon vanilla. In second large bowl, place chocolate chips and remaining 1 teaspoon vanilla. In large saucepan, stir together corn syrup and brown sugar; cook over medium heat, stirring constantly, until mixture comes to full, rolling boil. Remove from heat. Immediately pour half of hot mixture into each reserved bowl; stir each mixture until chips are melted and mixture is smooth. Immediately stir 6 cups rice cereal into each mixture. Spread peanut butter mixture into prepared pan; spread chocolate mixture on top of peanut butter layer. Cool completely. Use foil to lift treat out of pan; peel off foil. Cut treat into pieces. Store in tightly covered container in cool, dry place.

About 6 dozen pieces

Clockwise from top left: No-Bake Butterscotch Haystacks, Toffee Popcorn Crunch, Double-Decker Cereal Treats (page 205)

No-Bake Butterscotch Haystacks

1 cup HERSHEY'S
    Butterscotch Chips
½ cup REESE'S Peanut Butter
    Chips
1 tablespoon shortening (do
    not use butter, margarine
    or oil)

1½ cups (3-ounce can) chow
    mein noodles, coarsely
    broken

Line tray with wax paper. In medium microwave-safe bowl, place butterscotch chips, peanut butter chips and shortening. Microwave at HIGH (100%) 1 minute; stir. If necessary, microwave at HIGH an additional 15 seconds at a time, stirring after each heating, just until chips are melted when stirred. Immediately add chow mein noodles; stir to coat. Drop mixture by heaping teaspoonfuls onto prepared tray or into paper candy cups; let stand until firm. If necessary, cover and refrigerate until firm. Store in tightly covered container in refrigerator.

About 2 dozen candies

Toffee Popcorn Crunch

10 cups popped popcorn
 1 cup whole almonds
1¾ cups (10-ounce package)
    SKOR English Toffee Bits

⅔ cup light corn syrup

Heat oven to 275°F. Grease large roasting pan (*or* two 13×9×2-inch baking pans). Place popcorn and almonds in prepared pan. In heavy medium saucepan, combine toffee bits and corn syrup. Cook over medium heat, stirring constantly, until toffee is melted (about 12 minutes). Pour over popcorn mixture; stir until evenly coated. Bake 30 minutes, stirring frequently. Remove from oven; stir every 2 minutes until slightly cooled. Cool completely. Store in tightly covered container in cool, dry place.

About 1½ pounds popcorn

Note: *For best results, do* not *double this recipe.*

Royal Hot Chocolate

2 bars (1 ounce *each*)
    HERSHEY'S Unsweetened
    Baking Chocolate, broken
    into pieces
1 can (14 ounces) sweetened
    condensed milk (*not*
    evaporated milk)

4 cups boiling water
1 teaspoon vanilla extract
    Dash salt
    Whipped cream (optional)
    Ground cinnamon (optional)

In large heavy saucepan over very low heat, melt chocolate. Stir in sweetened condensed milk. Gradually add water, stirring until well blended. Stir in vanilla and salt. Garnish with whipped cream and cinnamon, if desired. Serve immediately.

8 servings

Mocha Shake

¼ cup warm water
2 tablespoons HERSHEY'S
    Cocoa
1 tablespoon sugar

1 to 2 teaspoons powdered
    instant coffee
½ cup milk
2 cups vanilla ice cream

In blender, place water, cocoa, sugar and instant coffee. Cover; blend briefly on low speed. Add milk. Cover; blend well on high speed until thoroughly blended. Add ice cream. Cover; blend until smooth. Serve immediately.

3 servings

Luscious Cocoa Smoothies

¼ cup HERSHEY'S Cocoa
2 tablespoons sugar
3 tablespoons warm water

1 banana, peeled and sliced
1½ cups skim milk
2 cups nonfat frozen yogurt

In small bowl, stir together cocoa and sugar. Add water; stir until well blended. In blender, place banana and cocoa mixture. Cover; blend until smooth. Add milk and frozen yogurt. Cover; blend until smooth. Serve immediately.

4 servings

Left to right: Royal Hot Chocolate, Mocha Shake, Luscious Cocoa Smoothie

Chocolate Peanut Butter Fudge

2 cups sugar
⅔ cup milk
3 bars (1 ounce *each*)
    HERSHEY'S Unsweetened
    Baking Chocolate, broken
    into pieces

1 cup marshmallow creme
¾ cup REESE'S Peanut Butter
1 teaspoon vanilla extract

Butter 9-inch square pan. In heavy 3-quart saucepan, stir together sugar, milk and chocolate. Cook over medium heat, stirring constantly, until mixture comes to full, rolling boil. Boil, without stirring, until mixture reaches 234°F on candy thermometer or until syrup, when dropped into very cold water, forms a soft ball that flattens when removed from water. (Bulb of thermometer should not rest on bottom of saucepan.) Remove from heat. Add marshmallow creme, peanut butter and vanilla; stir just until blended. Pour into prepared pan; cool until firm. Cut into squares. *About 3 dozen pieces*

Note: *For best results, do* not *double this recipe.*

Rich Cocoa Balls

4 cups (about 1 pound)
    powdered sugar, divided
¾ cup HERSHEY'S Cocoa
1 can (14 ounces) sweetened
    condensed milk (*not*
    evaporated milk)

1 tablespoon vanilla extract
2 cups finely chopped nuts

Reserve ½ cup powdered sugar for coating. In large bowl, stir together remaining 3½ cups powdered sugar and cocoa. Add sweetened condensed milk and vanilla. Beat on medium speed of electric mixer until blended, about 2 minutes. Stir in nuts. Cover; refrigerate 30 minutes or until mixture is firm enough to handle. Shape into 1-inch balls; roll in reserved ½ cup powdered sugar. Cover; refrigerate 2 hours or until firm. Store in refrigerator in tightly covered container.

About 5 dozen pieces

Rich Minty Cocoa Balls: *Omit nuts. Substitute ½ teaspoon peppermint extract for 1 tablespoon vanilla extract. Roll in crushed peppermint stick candy to coat.*

Chocolate Raspberry Fudge

2¼ cups sugar

1 cup plus 2 tablespoons (5-ounce can) evaporated milk

¼ cup (½ stick) butter or margarine

1⅔ cups (10-ounce package) HERSHEY'S Raspberry Chips

1 jar (7 ounces) marshmallow creme

1 teaspoon vanilla extract

Line 8- or 9-inch square pan with foil, extending foil over edges of pan. Butter foil lightly. In heavy 3-quart saucepan, stir together sugar, evaporated milk and butter. Cook over medium heat, stirring constantly, until mixture comes to full rolling boil; boil 5 minutes, stirring constantly. Remove from heat. Gradually add raspberry chips, stirring until melted. Add marshmallow creme and vanilla; stir until smooth. Pour into prepared pan; cool until firm. Use foil to lift fudge out of pan; peel off foil. Cut fudge into squares. Store in tightly covered container in cool, dry place.

About 4 dozen pieces or about 2 pounds fudge

Note: *For best results, do* not *double this recipe.*

Chocolate & Peanut Butter Dipped Apples

10 to 12 medium apples, stems
    removed
10 to 12 wooden ice cream
    sticks
1 cup HERSHEY'S Semi-Sweet
    Chocolate Chips
1⅔ cups (10-ounce package)
    REESE'S Peanut Butter
    Chips, divided

¼ cup plus 2 tablespoons
    shortening (do *not* use
    butter, margarine or oil),
    divided

Line tray with wax paper. Wash apples; dry thoroughly. Insert wooden stick into each apple; place on prepared tray. In medium microwave-safe bowl, place chocolate chips, ⅔ cup peanut butter chips and ¼ cup shortening. Microwave at HIGH (100%) 1 to 1½ minutes; stir. If necessary, microwave at HIGH an additional 30 seconds at a time, stirring after each heating, just until chips are melted when stirred. Dip bottom three-fourths of each apple into mixture. Twirl and shake gently to remove excess; return to prepared tray. In small microwave-safe bowl, place remaining 1 cup peanut butter chips and remaining 2 tablespoons shortening. Microwave at HIGH 30 seconds; stir. If necessary, microwave at HIGH an additional 30 seconds at a time, stirring after each heating, just until chips are melted and mixture is smooth when stirred. Spoon over top of each apple, allowing to drip down sides. Store in refrigerator.

10 to 12 coated apples

Chocolate & Peanut Butter Dipped Apples

LIGHT & LUSCIOUS

Luscious Chocolate Cheesecake

2 cups (1 pound) nonfat
  cottage cheese
¾ cup thawed frozen egg
  substitute
⅔ cup sugar
4 ounces (½ of 8-ounce
  package) Neufchâtel
  cheese, softened

⅓ cup HERSHEY'S Cocoa or
  HERSHEY'S European
  Style Cocoa
½ teaspoon vanilla extract
  Yogurt Topping (page 216)
  Sliced strawberries
  or mandarin orange
  segments (optional)

Heat oven to 300°F. Spray 9-inch springform pan with vegetable cooking spray. In food processor, place cottage cheese, egg substitute, sugar, Neufchâtel cheese, cocoa and vanilla; process until smooth. Pour into prepared pan. Bake 35 minutes or until edge is set. Meanwhile, prepare Yogurt Topping; carefully spread topping over cheesecake. Continue baking 5 minutes. Remove from oven to wire rack. With knife, immediately loosen cheesecake from side of pan. Cool completely. Cover; refrigerate until chilled. Just before serving, remove side of pan. Serve with strawberries or oranges, if desired. Refrigerate leftover cheesecake.   *12 servings*

continued on page 216

Luscious Chocolate Cheesecake

Luscious Chocolate Cheesecake (continued)

Yogurt Topping

⅔ **cup plain nonfat yogurt**   **2 tablespoons sugar**

In small bowl, stir together yogurt and sugar until well blended.

Nutritional Information Per Serving		
120 Calories	3 g Fat	210 mg Sodium
8 g Protein	10 mg Cholesterol	60 mg Calcium
17 g Carbohydrate		

Sinfully Rich Nonfat Fudge Sauce

½ **cup sugar**
¼ **cup HERSHEY'S Cocoa or**
  HERSHEY'S European
  Style Cocoa
1 **tablespoon plus 1 teaspoon**
  cornstarch
½ **cup evaporated skim milk**

2 **teaspoons vanilla extract**
  Assorted fresh fruit
  (optional)
Cake (optional)
Frozen nonfat yogurt
  (optional)

In small saucepan, stir together sugar, cocoa and cornstarch; stir in evaporated milk. Cook over low heat, stirring constantly, until mixture comes to boil; continue cooking until sauce is smooth and thickened, stirring constantly. Remove from heat. Stir in vanilla. Serve warm or cold with fresh fruit, cake or frozen nonfat yogurt, if desired. Cover; refrigerate leftover sauce.   *7 servings*

Nutritional Information Per Serving (2 tablespoons sauce)		
80 Calories	0 g Fat	25 mg Sodium
2 g Protein	0 mg Cholesterol	55 mg Calcium
19 g Carbohydrate		

Mini Brownie Cups

¼ cup (½ stick) corn oil spread (60% oil)
2 egg whites
1 egg
¾ cup sugar

⅔ cup all-purpose flour
⅓ cup HERSHEY'S Cocoa
½ teaspoon baking powder
¼ teaspoon salt
Mocha Glaze (recipe follows)

Heat oven to 350°F. Line small muffin cups (1¾ inches in diameter) with paper bake cups or spray with vegetable cooking spray. In small saucepan over low heat, melt corn oil spread; cool slightly. In small mixer bowl on medium speed of electric mixer, beat egg whites and egg until foamy; gradually add sugar, beating until slightly thickened and light in color. Stir together flour, cocoa, baking powder and salt; gradually add to egg mixture, beating until blended. Gradually add corn oil spread, beating just until blended. Fill muffin cups ⅔ full with batter. Bake 15 to 18 minutes or until wooden pick inserted in center comes out clean. Remove from pan to wire rack. Cool completely. Prepare Mocha Glaze; drizzle over tops of brownie cups. Let stand until glaze is set.   *24 servings*

Mocha Glaze

¼ cup powdered sugar
¾ teaspoon HERSHEY'S Cocoa
¼ teaspoon powdered instant coffee

2 teaspoons hot water
¼ teaspoon vanilla extract

In small bowl, stir together powdered sugar and cocoa. Dissolve coffee in water; gradually add to sugar mixture, stirring until well blended. Stir in vanilla.

Nutritional Information Per Serving (1 brownie cup)		
60 Calories	2 g Fat	50 mg Sodium
1 g Protein	10 mg Cholesterol	5 mg Calcium
10 g Carbohydrate		

Fruit-Filled Chocolate Dreams

Fruit-Filled Chocolate Dreams

1 envelope (1.3 ounces) dry
    whipped topping mix
1 tablespoon HERSHEY'S
    Cocoa
½ cup cold skim milk

½ teaspoon vanilla extract
Dreamy Chocolate Sauce
    (recipe follows)
Assorted fresh fruit, cut up

Line cookie sheet with foil. In small, deep mixer bowl with narrow bottom, stir together topping mix and cocoa. Add milk and vanilla; beat on high speed of electric mixer until stiff peaks form. Spoon topping into five mounds onto prepared cookie sheet. With spoon, shape each mound into 4-inch shell. Freeze about 1 hour or until firm. Meanwhile, prepare Dreamy Chocolate Sauce. To serve, fill center of each frozen shell with about ⅓ cup assorted fresh fruit; drizzle with 1 tablespoon prepared sauce. Serve immediately.   *5 servings*

Dreamy Chocolate Sauce

¾ cup sugar
⅓ cup HERSHEY'S Cocoa
1 tablespoon cornstarch

¾ cup water
1 tablespoon margarine
1 teaspoon vanilla extract

In small saucepan, combine sugar, cocoa and cornstarch; gradually stir in water. Cook over medium heat, stirring constantly, until mixture comes to a boil; boil 1 minute. Remove from heat. Add margarine and vanilla; stir until smooth. Cover; refrigerate until cold.

Nutritional Information Per Serving		
130 Calories	1 g Fat	25 mg Sodium
2 g Protein	0 mg Cholesterol	45 mg Calcium
27 g Carbohydrate		

Chocolate Roulade with Creamy Yogurt Filling

Creamy Yogurt Filling
  (page 222)
3 egg whites
½ cup granulated sugar,
  divided
1 container (8 ounces) frozen
  egg substitute, thawed
½ cup cake flour

¼ cup HERSHEY'S Cocoa
1 teaspoon baking powder
⅛ teaspoon salt
2 tablespoons water
1 teaspoon vanilla extract
2 teaspoons powdered sugar
  Peach Sauce (page 222)

Prepare Creamy Yogurt Filling. Heat oven to 375°F. Line 15½×10½×1-inch jelly-roll pan with foil; spray with vegetable cooking spray. In large mixer bowl on medium speed of electric mixer, beat egg whites until foamy; gradually add ¼ cup granulated sugar, beating on high speed until stiff peaks form. In small mixer bowl, beat egg substitute on medium speed until foamy; gradually add remaining ¼ cup granulated sugar, beating until mixture is thick. Fold egg substitute mixture into egg whites. Stir together flour, cocoa, baking powder and salt; add alternately with combined water and vanilla to egg mixture, folding after each addition until blended. Spread batter into prepared pan. Bake 10 to 12 minutes or until top springs back when touched lightly. Immediately invert onto towel sprinkled with powdered sugar; peel off foil. Starting at narrow end, roll cake and towel together. Cool completely on wire rack. Unroll cake; remove towel. Spread cake with prepared filling to within ½ inch of edges of cake. Reroll cake; place, seam side down, on serving plate. Cover; refrigerate 2 to 3 hours or until chilled. Meanwhile, prepare Peach Sauce. Slice cake; serve with prepared sauce. Garnish as desired.

10 servings

Note: *Cake is best when eaten same day as prepared.*

continued on page 222

Chocolate Roulade with Creamy Yogurt Filling

Chocolate Roulade with Creamy Yogurt Filling (continued)

Creamy Yogurt Filling

Yogurt Cheese (recipe
follows)
1 envelope (1.3 ounces) dry
whipped topping mix

⅓ cup cold skim milk
1 teaspoon vanilla extract
⅛ to ¼ teaspoon almond
extract

Prepare Yogurt Cheese. In small, deep mixer bowl with narrow-bottom, place topping mix. Add ⅓ cup milk, 1 teaspoon vanilla and almond extract; beat on high speed of electric mixer until stiff peaks form. Fold prepared Yogurt Cheese into whipped topping.

Yogurt Cheese

1 container (8 ounces) plain
lowfat yogurt, no gelatin
added

Line non-rusting colander or sieve with large piece of double thickness cheesecloth or large coffee filter; place colander over deep bowl. Spoon yogurt into prepared colander; cover with plastic wrap. Refrigerate until liquid no longer drains from yogurt, about 24 hours. Remove yogurt from cheesecloth. Place in separate bowl; discard liquid.

Peach Sauce

1½ cups fresh peach slices
1 tablespoon sugar

¼ cup water
1½ teaspoons cornstarch

In blender container, place peach slices and sugar. Cover; blend until smooth. In medium microwave-safe bowl, place water and cornstarch; stir until cornstarch is dissolved. Add peach mixture; stir. Microwave at HIGH (100%) 2½ minutes or until mixture comes to a boil and thickens, stirring after each minute. Cool completely.

Nutritional Information Per Serving					
140	Calories	1 g	Fat	130 mg	Sodium
6 g	Protein	0 mg	Cholesterol	65 mg	Calcium
26 g	Carbohydrate				

Choco-Lowfat Muffins

1½ cups all-purpose flour
¾ cup granulated sugar
¼ cup **HERSHEY'S Cocoa** or
    HERSHEY'S European
    Style Cocoa
2 teaspoons baking powder

1 teaspoon baking soda
½ teaspoon salt
⅔ cup lowfat vanilla yogurt
⅔ cup skim milk
½ teaspoon vanilla extract
    Powdered sugar (optional)

Heat oven to 400°F. Line muffin cups (2½ inches in diameter) with paper bake cups. In medium bowl, stir together flour, granulated sugar, cocoa, baking powder, baking soda and salt; stir in yogurt, milk and vanilla just until dry ingredients are moistened. *Do not beat.* Fill muffin cups ⅔ full with batter. Bake 15 to 20 minutes or until wooden pick inserted in center comes out clean. Cool slightly. Remove from pans to wire racks. Sift powdered sugar over tops of muffins, if desired. Serve warm. *14 muffins*

Nutritional Information Per Serving (1 muffin)					
100	Calories	1 g	Fat	200 mg	Sodium
2 g	Protein	0 mg	Cholesterol	45 mg	Calcium
22 g	Carbohydrate				

Hershey's Slimmed Down Chocolate Cake

Hershey's Slimmed Down Chocolate Cake

6 tablespoons lower fat
   margarine (40% oil)
1 cup sugar
1 cup skim milk
1 tablespoon white vinegar
½ teaspoon vanilla extract

1¼ cups all-purpose flour
⅓ cup HERSHEY'S Cocoa
1 teaspoon baking soda
Slimmed Down Cocoa
   Frosting (recipe follows)

Heat oven to 350°F. Spray two 8-inch round baking pans with vegetable cooking spray. In medium saucepan over low heat, melt margarine; stir in sugar. Remove from heat. Add milk, vinegar and vanilla; stir until blended. Stir together flour, cocoa and baking soda. Add to sugar mixture; stir with whisk until well blended. Pour batter evenly into prepared pans. Bake 20 minutes or until wooden pick inserted in center comes out clean. Cool 10 minutes; remove from pans to wire racks. Cool completely. Prepare Slimmed Down Cocoa Frosting. Place one cake layer on serving plate; spread with half the prepared frosting. Place second cake layer on top; spread remaining frosting over top of cake. Refrigerate 2 to 3 hours or until chilled. Garnish as desired. Cover; refrigerate leftover cake.   *12 servings*

Slimmed Down Cocoa Frosting

1 envelope (1.3 ounces) dry
   whipped topping mix
1 tablespoon HERSHEY'S
  Cocoa

½ cup cold skim milk
½ teaspoon vanilla extract

In small, deep mixer bowl with narrow bottom, stir together topping mix and cocoa. Add ½ cup milk and ½ teaspoon vanilla. Beat on high speed of electric mixer 4 minutes or until soft peaks form.

Almond Frosting: *Omit ½ teaspoon vanilla extract. Add ¼ teaspoon almond extract.*

Nutritional Information Per Serving					
160	Calories	4 g	Fat	115 mg	Sodium
3 g	Protein	0 mg	Cholesterol	45 mg	Calcium
28 g	Carbohydrate				

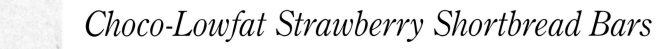

Choco-Lowfat Strawberry Shortbread Bars

¼ cup (½ stick) corn oil spread
    (60% oil)
½ cup sugar
1 egg white
1¼ cups all-purpose flour
¼ cup HERSHEY'S Cocoa or
    HERSHEY'S European
    Style Cocoa

¾ teaspoon cream of tartar
½ teaspoon baking soda
    Dash salt
½ cup strawberry all-fruit
    spread
    Vanilla Chip Drizzle (recipe
    follows)

Heat oven to 375°F. Lightly spray 13×9×2-inch baking pan with vegetable cooking spray. In medium mixer bowl, combine corn oil spread and sugar; beat on medium speed of electric mixer until well blended. Add egg white; beat until well blended. Stir together flour, cocoa, cream of tartar, baking soda and salt; gradually add to sugar mixture, beating well. Gently press mixture onto bottom of prepared pan. Bake 10 to 12 minutes or just until set. Cool completely in pan on wire rack. Spread fruit spread over crust. Cut into bars or other desired shapes with cookie cutters. Prepare Vanilla Chip Drizzle; drizzle over tops of bars. Let stand until drizzle is set. *36 bars*

Vanilla Chip Drizzle

⅓ cup HERSHEY'S Vanilla
    Milk Chips

½ teaspoon shortening (do
    not use butter, margarine
    or oil)

In small microwave-safe bowl, place vanilla milk chips and shortening. Microwave at HIGH (100%) 30 seconds; stir. If necessary, microwave at HIGH an additional 15 seconds at a time, stirring after each heating, just until chips are melted when stirred. Use immediately.

Nutritional Information Per Serving (1 bar)					
50	Calories	1 g	Fat	45 mg	Sodium
1 g	Protein	0 mg	Cholesterol	5 mg	Calcium
10 g	Carbohydrate				

Choco-Lowfat Strawberry Shortbread Bars

Chocolate Cherry Angel Delight

⅓ cup HERSHEY'S Cocoa
1 package (about 15 ounces) "two-step" angel food cake mix
1 envelope (1.3 ounces) dry whipped topping mix

½ cup cold skim milk
½ teaspoon vanilla extract
1 can (20 ounces) reduced-calorie cherry pie filling, chilled

Move oven rack to lowest position. In small bowl, sift cocoa over contents of cake flour packet; stir to blend. Proceed with mixing cake as directed on package. Bake and cool as directed for 10-inch tube pan. Carefully run knife along side of pan to loosen cake; remove from pan. Using serrated knife, slice cake horizontally into three layers. In small, deep mixer bowl with narrow bottom, place topping mix. Add ½ cup milk and ½ teaspoon vanilla; beat on high speed of electric mixer until stiff peaks form. Fold half the pie filling into whipped topping. Place bottom cake layer on serving plate; spread with half the whipped topping mixture. Repeat layers, ending with plain cake layer on top. Spoon remaining pie filling over top. Serve immediately. Cover; refrigerate leftover cake.   *14 servings*

Nutritional Information Per Serving		
170 Calories	0 g Fat	135 mg Sodium
4 g Protein	0 mg Cholesterol	15 mg Calcium
39 g Carbohydrate		

Chocolate Mousse Squares

¾ cup plus 2 tablespoons all-purpose flour, divided
3 tablespoons plus ⅔ cup granulated sugar, divided
¼ cup (½ stick) cold margarine
¼ cup HERSHEY'S Cocoa
½ teaspoon powdered instant coffee

¼ teaspoon baking powder
½ cup thawed frozen egg substitute
½ teaspoon vanilla extract
½ cup plain lowfat yogurt
½ teaspoon powdered sugar

Heat oven to 350°F. In medium bowl, stir together ¾ cup flour and 3 tablespoons granulated sugar. With pastry blender, cut in margarine until mixture resembles fine crumbs. Press mixture onto bottom of ungreased 8-inch square baking pan. Bake 15 minutes or until golden. Remove from oven. *Reduce oven temperature to 300°F.* Meanwhile, in small mixer bowl, stir together remaining ⅔ cup granulated sugar, cocoa, remaining 2 tablespoons flour, instant coffee and baking powder. Add egg substitute and vanilla; beat on medium speed of electric mixer until well blended. Add yogurt; beat just until blended. Pour over prepared crust. Bake 30 minutes or until almost set in center. Cool completely in pan on wire rack. Sift powdered sugar over top. Cut into 2-inch squares. Cover; refrigerate leftover squares.

16 squares

Nutritional Information Per Serving (1 square)		
100 Calories	3 g Fat	55 mg Sodium
2 g Protein	0 mg Cholesterol	20 mg Calcium
16 g Carbohydrate		

Crispy Cocoa Bars

¼ cup (½ stick) margarine
¼ cup HERSHEY'S Cocoa
5 cups miniature marshmallows

5 cups crisp rice cereal

Spray 13×9×2-inch pan with vegetable cooking spray. In large saucepan over low heat, melt margarine; stir in cocoa and marshmallows. Cook over low heat, stirring constantly, until marshmallows are melted and mixture is smooth and well blended. Continue cooking 1 minute, stirring constantly. Remove from heat. Add cereal; stir until evenly coated. Lightly spray spatula with vegetable cooking spray; press mixture into prepared pan. Cool completely. Cut into bars.

24 bars

Nutritional Information Per Serving (1 bar)		
90 Calories	2 g Fat	100 mg Sodium
1 g Protein	0 mg Cholesterol	5 mg Calcium
16 g Carbohydrate		

INDEX

METRIC CONVERSION CHART

VOLUME MEASUREMENTS (dry)

1/8 teaspoon = 0.5 mL
1/4 teaspoon = 1 mL
1/2 teaspoon = 2 mL
3/4 teaspoon = 4 mL
1 teaspoon = 5 mL
1 tablespoon = 15 mL
2 tablespoons = 30 mL
1/4 cup = 60 mL
1/3 cup = 75 mL
1/2 cup = 125 mL
2/3 cup = 150 mL
3/4 cup = 175 mL
1 cup = 250 mL
2 cups = 1 pint = 500 mL
3 cups = 750 mL
4 cups = 1 quart = 1 L

VOLUME MEASUREMENTS (fluid)

1 fluid ounce (2 tablespoons) = 30 mL
4 fluid ounces (1/2 cup) = 125 mL
8 fluid ounces (1 cup) = 250 mL
12 fluid ounces (1 1/2 cups) = 375 mL
16 fluid ounces (2 cups) = 500 mL

WEIGHTS (mass)

1/2 ounce = 15 g
1 ounce = 30 g
3 ounces = 90 g
4 ounces = 120 g
8 ounces = 225 g
10 ounces = 285 g
12 ounces = 360 g
16 ounces = 1 pound = 450 g

DIMENSIONS

1/16 inch = 2 mm
1/8 inch = 3 mm
1/4 inch = 6 mm
1/2 inch = 1.5 cm
3/4 inch = 2 cm
1 inch = 2.5 cm

OVEN TEMPERATURES

250°F = 120°C
275°F = 140°C
300°F = 150°C
325°F = 160°C
350°F = 180°C
375°F = 190°C
400°F = 200°C
425°F = 220°C
450°F = 230°C

BAKING PAN SIZES

Utensil	Size in Inches/Quarts	Metric Volume	Size in Centimeters
Baking or Cake pan (square or rectangular)	8×8×2	2 L	20×20×5
	9×9×2	2.5 L	22×22×5
	12×8×2	3 L	30×20×5
	13×9×2	3.5 L	33×23×5
Loaf Pan	8×4×3	1.5 L	20×10×7
	9×5×3	2 L	23×13×7
Round Layer Cake Pan	8×1½	1.2 L	20×4
	9×1½	1.5 L	23×4
Pie Plate	8×1¼	750 mL	20×3
	9×1¼	1 L	23×3
Baking Dish or Casserole	1 quart	1 L	—
	1½ quart	1.5 L	—
	2 quart	2 L	—